Middle School Trials

Roseanne Godkin

Published by Roseanne Godkin, 2024.

While every precaution has been taken in the preparation of this book, the publisher assumes no responsibility for errors or omissions, or for damages resulting from the use of the information contained herein.

MIDDLE SCHOOL TRIALS

First edition. October 21, 2024.

Copyright © 2024 Roseanne Godkin.

ISBN: 979-8227703422

Written by Roseanne Godkin.

About the Author

Roseanne a dedicated Middle and High school History and Psychology Teacher, drew inspiration from her students' daily adventures and growth. Capturing their humor and challenges, she penned "Nathan's Middle School Adventures". Through this book, filled with laughter and warmth,

Roseanne celebrated the journey of adolescence, reminding her students that navigating friendships and discovering passions are part of the joyous chaos of growing up. Her storytelling not only entertained but also fostered empathy and connection in her classroom, making her students feel seen and understood in their middle school escapades.

Read her other book 'Echoes of Shadows and Light in Pig's Inn Village'

Acknowledgements

To my wonderful Braestars,

As I reflect on our time together, I'm overwhelmed with gratitude for each of you. Your enthusiasm, curiosity, and resilience have inspired me beyond words. Writing "Nathan's Middle School Adventures" was a joy because it allowed me to capture the laughter and lessons we shared in our classroom. You are the heart of this book, and I hope it brings a smile to your faces as it did to mine.

To my colleagues at Braestar,

Working alongside such dedicated educators was a privilege. Your support and collaboration made every day at Braestar a rewarding experience. Thank you for your friendship, wisdom, and endless encouragement. Together, we created a nurturing environment where students thrived and dreams took flight.

To my family and all my sisters

Your unwavering support and understanding have been my anchor throughout this journey. From late nights writing to weekends lost in edits, you've been my biggest cheerleaders. Thank you for believing in me and for being my constant source of love and inspiration.

With sincere appreciation,

Roseanne Godkin

Prologue

Welcome to the whirlwind world of Nathan's middle school adventures! From sticky cafeteria dilemmas to epic Nerf battles and glittery science mishaps, Nathan's journey through the halls of adolescence is anything but ordinary. Join him as he navigates friendships, survives detentions, and discovers that sometimes, the greatest lessons come from the most unexpected places.

Filled with humor, heart, and a cast of unforgettable characters—including loyal friends Zack and Gabe, the indomitable Principal Allen, and the no-nonsense Miss. Erin—Nathan's Middle School Adventures is a delightful romp through the ups and downs of growing up. Perfect for readers of all ages looking for laughter, life lessons, and the joy of embracing every moment, this book is a testament to the resilience and spirit that define the middle school experience.

Introduction:

Nathan's Summer Dreams and Middle School Realities

SUMMER HOLIDAYS WERE supposed to be long and fun, a time Nathan eagerly anticipated every year. He had grand plans to visit his friends and have extended sleepovers, provided his parents permitted it. However, his mum was particularly unenthusiastic about these sleepovers. She often said, "Nathan, you don't know what rituals some parents have at night! And what is it that you will do in the night—sleeping?" Because of this, Nathan never got to experience what some boys in his class called "the fantastic night."

Despite this, Nathan looked forward to summer with hopes of camping at 'Rapids Camp Sagana', a popular spot among his schoolmates. He had heard countless stories about the numerous activities there from those fortunate enough to have camped. The highlight for him was white water rafting. He imagined the thrill of navigating the fast-flowing, rough river with water crashing against the rocks. White water rafting was described as an adrenaline-filled experience, with a series of exciting rapids that provided thrills and challenges for rafters for hours or even a whole day. The river meandered through lush forests, rocky gorges, and scenic valleys, offering breathtaking views along the way.

In addition to white water rafting, Nathan dreamed of trying kayaking, zip-lining, archery, and rock climbing. The prospect of these adventures filled him with excitement, and he couldn't wait for the summer to begin.

However, despite his excitement, Nathan couldn't shake off the looming thoughts of starting middle school. These thoughts cast a shadow over his summer dreams, making the break seem dull even

MIDDLE SCHOOL TRIALS

before it began. Middle school was a whole new world, filled with unknowns and challenges that Nathan wasn't sure he was ready to face.

As the summer approached, Nathan realized that he needed to make the most of his holiday while preparing himself mentally for the transition to middle school. He decided that this summer would be different. He would balance his adventurous plans with moments of reflection and preparation for the new school year. This book is Nathan's journey through the ups and downs of middle school, filled with real experiences, challenges, and the lessons he learned along the way.

Join Nathan as he navigates the complexities of middle school life, deals with the "middle school crap," and discovers that growing up, while daunting, can also be an incredible adventure. Whether you're about to start middle school or are already in the thick of it, Nathan's story will resonate with you, offering insights, tips, and a sense of camaraderie as you face your own middle school journey.

Chapter 1: The First Day Jitters

Nathan's heart pounded as he stood in front of the large, imposing building that was his new middle school. The summer had flown by, and now the day he had both dreaded and eagerly anticipated was finally here. Clutching his backpack, he took a deep breath and stepped forward, determined to face whatever challenges lay ahead.

As he walked through the doors, the cacophony of voices, the sea of unfamiliar faces, and the maze of hallways overwhelmed him. He glanced at his schedule, trying to make sense of the room numbers and teacher names. In all the years before, Nathan only needed to know his class teacher, the games and swimming teacher which was a bliss. Understanding the new environment seemed like a foreign language.

His first class was science with Mr. Calvin. Navigating the crowded hallways, he finally found the room and slipped into a seat near the back. He scanned the room, noticing the confident chatter of students who seemed to already know each other. Nathan felt a pang of loneliness but reminded himself that everyone was new to middle school at some point.

Mr. Calvin, a tall man with a kind smile, began the class with an icebreaker activity. "Let's start by sharing one interesting fact about ourselves," he said. Nathan's mind raced. What could he share that wouldn't make him seem boring or weird?

When it was his turn, he stood up, his palms sweaty. "Hi, I'm Nathan," he began, his voice wavering. "I love outdoor adventures, like camping and white water rafting." There was a murmur of interest, and a few students nodded approvingly. Feeling a bit more at ease, Nathan sat down, relieved that he had survived his first class.

MIDDLE SCHOOL TRIALS

Between classes, Nathan wandered the hallways, trying to find his next destination. The school map he'd been given at orientation felt like a treasure map with no clear path. He spotted a friendly-looking girl and mustered the courage to ask for directions.

"Hi, I'm Nathan. Do you know where Room 204 is?" he asked.

"Sure, I'm Emily," she replied with a smile. "I'm headed that way too. Let's go together."

As they walked, Emily chatted about the different clubs and activities available at the school. Nathan felt a flicker of excitement. Maybe joining a club could help him meet new friends and find his place in this new environment.

By lunchtime, Nathan had successfully navigated through a few more classes. He made his way to the cafeteria, which was buzzing with energy. The daunting task of finding a place to sit loomed ahead. He scanned the room, hoping to spot a familiar face. Just as he was about to resign himself to eating alone, he heard a voice.

"Hey, Nathan! Over here!" It was Emily, waving him over to a table where she sat with a few other students. Grateful, Nathan joined them, introducing himself to the others. They exchanged stories about their summer and their first impressions of middle school. For the first time that day, Nathan felt a sense of belonging.

The afternoon passed more smoothly. With each class, Nathan grew more confident in finding his way and speaking up. By the end of the day, he realized that while middle school was a big, unfamiliar place, it wasn't as intimidating as he had imagined. He had met a few friendly faces and was starting to find his footing.

As he walked home, Nathan thought about the day's events. He had navigated new environments, both physically and socially, and had come out the other side feeling more confident. He knew there would be more challenges ahead, but he was ready to face them. Middle school, with all its unknowns, was an adventure waiting to unfold, and Nathan was prepared to navigate it one step at a time.

The first few weeks of middle school were a whirlwind for Nathan. Despite finding his way around and making a few friends, he couldn't shake the feeling of anxiety that clung to him like a shadow. Every morning, as he prepared for school, his stomach churned with nerves. Would he remember his locker combination? Would he be able to keep up with the schoolwork? What if he said something embarrassing in class?

One particularly stressful day began with Nathan waking up late. In his rush to get ready, he spilled toothpaste on his shirt and had to change. By the time he arrived at school, he was frazzled and barely made it to his first class on time. During math, he couldn't focus. His mind was a jumble of worries, and the numbers on the board seemed to blur together.

When the teacher called on him to solve a problem, his heart raced. "Nathan, can you come up and show us how to solve this equation?" Mr. Adam asked. His mind went blank, and he felt every pair of eyes in the room turn toward him. He stumbled to the front, his palms sweaty, and stared at the board, his anxiety escalating with each passing second.

"I'm sorry, I don't know," he finally muttered, his voice barely audible. Mr. Adam nodded understandingly and asked another student to help. Nathan returned to his seat, his cheeks burning with embarrassment. The rest of the class passed in a blur, and by the time the bell rang, he felt utterly defeated.

At lunch, Nathan sat with Emily and her friends, but he could barely eat. The morning's events replayed in his mind, amplifying his anxiety.

MIDDLE SCHOOL TRIALS

Emily noticed his distress and leaned in. "Hey, are you okay?" she asked gently.

Nathan shrugged. "Just having a rough day, I guess."

Emily gave him a sympathetic look. "I get it. Middle school is a lot to handle. Do you want to talk about it?"

Taking a deep breath, Nathan opened up about his worries—the fear of messing up in class, the overwhelming feeling of being in a new environment, and the constant anxiety that followed him. Emily listened patiently, nodding in understanding.

"You know," she said after he finished, "everyone feels nervous sometimes. It's totally normal. But there are things you can do to help manage it."

Nathan looked at her curiously. "Like what?"

"Well," Emily began, "my older brother taught me a few tricks. One thing that helps is deep breathing. When you start to feel anxious, try taking slow, deep breaths. It can really calm you down. Also, it helps to break things down into smaller steps. Focus on one thing at a time instead of everything all at once."

Nathan nodded, considering her advice. That afternoon, he decided to put it into practice. During his history class, when he felt a wave of anxiety approaching, he closed his eyes and took a few deep breaths. Inhale, hold, exhale. Gradually, his racing heart slowed, and he felt more grounded.

After school, Nathan went home and talked to his parents about his anxiety. They were supportive and suggested he try writing in a journal. That evening, Nathan sat down with a notebook and began to jot down his thoughts and feelings. It was a simple act, but it felt like a weight was being lifted off his shoulders with each word he wrote.

Over the next few weeks, Nathan continued to practice these techniques. He reminded himself to breathe deeply when he felt overwhelmed, broke tasks into manageable steps, and wrote in his journal regularly. Slowly but surely, he began to notice a difference. While the anxiety didn't disappear completely, it became more manageable.

One day, during a particularly challenging science lab, Nathan felt the familiar stirrings of nervousness. Instead of letting it take over, he paused, took a deep breath, and approached the task step by step. By the end of the lab, he felt a sense of accomplishment. He had faced his anxiety head-on and emerged stronger.

Nathan realized that dealing with anxiety was a journey, one that required patience and persistence. It was okay to feel nervous, and it was okay to ask for help. With each small victory, he gained more confidence in his ability to navigate middle school and all the challenges it brought.

As he continued to face new situations and uncertainties, Nathan learned that while anxiety might be a part of his life, it didn't have to control it. He was equipped with the tools to manage it and the support of friends and family to help him along the way. Middle school was still an adventure, and Nathan was ready to embrace it, one breath at a time.

As Nathan settled into the routine of middle school, he quickly realized that one of the most daunting tasks was meeting new people and making friends. While he had a few acquaintances like Emily, he yearned for a close-knit group of friends who would make his middle school experience more enjoyable.

MIDDLE SCHOOL TRIALS

It was during his second week of school that Nathan's homeroom teacher, Miss. Martina, announced a group project. The assignment was to create a presentation on an ecosystem, and Miss. Martina assigned the groups randomly. Nathan found himself grouped with three other students: Lucas, a quiet boy who always seemed to be drawing; Mia, an energetic girl who was always surrounded by friends; and Ben, a sports enthusiast who seemed to know everyone.

Nathan felt a mix of excitement and apprehension. He wanted to make a good impression but wasn't sure how to start a conversation with his new groupmates. After class, the group decided to meet in the library to discuss their project.

As they sat down, Mia took charge. "Okay, so we need to decide on an ecosystem. Any ideas?"

"I was thinking the Amazon Rainforest," Ben suggested. "There's so much we can cover, from the animals to the plants."

Nathan nodded, trying to contribute. "I've read that the Amazon Rainforest produces a significant amount of the world's oxygen. We could talk about its importance to the global environment."

"That's a great idea," Lucas said, looking up from his sketchbook. "I can draw some illustrations for our presentation."

The ice was broken, and the group started to collaborate more comfortably. Nathan found that contributing his ideas and listening to others was a good way to build rapport. As they discussed their project, he learned more about his groupmates. Lucas loved art and was incredibly talented at drawing. Mia was passionate about theater and was involved in the school's drama club. Ben played soccer and was excited about the upcoming tryouts.

Working on the project together, Nathan discovered that making friends was about finding common ground and showing genuine interest in others. As they divided the tasks, they also shared stories and laughed about their middle school experiences so far. Nathan felt a sense of camaraderie growing within the group.

One day, as they were wrapping up their meeting, Ben turned to Nathan. "Hey, do you play any sports?"

Nathan hesitated. "Not really, but I like outdoor activities like camping and rafting."

"That's cool," Ben said. "You should come to the soccer tryouts with me. It's fun, even if you've never played before."

Nathan felt a surge of nervousness but also excitement. "Sure, I'll give it a try."

The next day, Nathan showed up at the soccer field. Ben introduced him to the other players, and Nathan felt a bit out of place at first. However, as the practice went on, he found himself enjoying the game. Ben was encouraging, and the other players were friendly and welcoming.

Over the next few weeks, Nathan started to bond more with Ben, Lucas, and Mia. They spent time together outside of their project, eating lunch together and hanging out after school. Mia invited Nathan to watch a rehearsal of the school play, and he was amazed by her acting skills. Lucas shared some of his drawings with Nathan, who admired his talent. Ben and Nathan continued to practice soccer together, and Nathan found himself getting better at the sport.

One afternoon, after a particularly intense soccer practice, Nathan and Ben sat on the bleachers, catching their breath.

MIDDLE SCHOOL TRIALS

"You did great today," Ben said, giving Nathan a thumbs-up.

"Thanks," Nathan replied, smiling. "I'm really starting to enjoy soccer. And it's nice having friends to hang out with."

Ben nodded. "Yeah, middle school's a lot better when you have people to share it with."

Nathan realized how true that was. Meeting new people and making friends had seemed intimidating at first, but by being open, contributing to group activities, and showing interest in others, he had started to build meaningful friendships.

As the school year progressed, Nathan's circle of friends continued to grow. He joined Mia's drama club, participated in art projects with Lucas, and became a regular at soccer practices with Ben. Each new connection enriched his middle school experience, making the challenges more manageable and the good times even better.

Nathan learned that making friends wasn't about being the most outgoing or popular person; it was about being yourself, showing kindness, and being open to new experiences. With this newfound confidence, he felt ready to tackle whatever middle school had in store for him, surrounded by friends who supported and encouraged him every step of the way.

Chapter 2: Navigating Social Circles

Middle school is a melting pot of personalities, interests, and backgrounds. For Nathan, this meant navigating a landscape filled with diverse social groups. Understanding these different circles was essential for finding where he fit in and building meaningful relationships.

During the first few weeks, Nathan observed the various groups in the school. There were the athletes who spent their free time on the sports fields, the theater kids who could be found rehearsing lines in the auditorium, the artists who carried sketchbooks and talked about their latest projects, and the academically focused students who were often seen in the library, engrossed in their studies. Each group had its own dynamic and unspoken rules.

One morning, as Nathan walked into the cafeteria, he noticed these groups more clearly. The athletes, including his friend Ben, dominated one corner, their loud conversations and easy camaraderie marking them as a tight-knit bunch. Nearby, Mia sat with the theater kids, animatedly discussing the latest play. Lucas was at a table with other artists, sketching and exchanging ideas. Nathan felt a bit overwhelmed by the distinct social circles but reminded himself that it was okay to explore and find his place.

Nathan knew he didn't have to belong to just one group. He had interests that spanned across multiple circles, and he wanted to connect with different kinds of people. He decided to approach socializing by finding common ground with others.

He started with Ben and the athletes. Although Nathan wasn't a star player, he enjoyed the physical activity and the sense of team spirit.

MIDDLE SCHOOL TRIALS

At soccer practice, he made an effort to engage with the other players, asking about their favorite sports teams and sharing his outdoor adventures. Over time, he felt more comfortable and accepted within the group.

Next, he explored his interest in the arts. One day after school, he approached Lucas and the artists. "Hey, can I join you guys?" he asked, feeling a bit nervous.

"Of course!" Lucas said, smiling. "We're just working on some sketches. Do you like to draw?"

"I'm not great at drawing, but I love being creative," Nathan admitted. "I'm interested in photography and capturing nature."

The artists welcomed him, and Nathan found himself inspired by their passion and talent. He started bringing his camera to school, sharing his photos with the group and learning new techniques from them. He discovered that artistic expression came in many forms, and his contributions were valued.

As Nathan continued to navigate the social circles, he realized the importance of being open to new experiences. When Mia invited him to join the drama club, he hesitated at first. Acting wasn't something he had ever considered, but he decided to give it a try.

At the first rehearsal, Nathan felt out of his element. The theater kids were lively and expressive, and he wasn't sure he could match their energy. But Mia encouraged him, and the director gave him a small role in the play. To his surprise, Nathan found joy in the collaborative process of putting on a performance. He learned to project his voice, express emotions, and work as part of a team. The experience broadened his perspective and helped him appreciate the dedication and talent of his theater friends.

As Nathan became more involved in different groups, he faced the challenge of balancing his time and energy. He didn't want to neglect any of his friends or commitments. He learned to manage his schedule, setting aside time for soccer practice, art sessions, and drama rehearsals. By being organized and communicating openly with his friends, he was able to maintain his connections and enjoy the best of all worlds.

Through his journey, Nathan discovered that true friendships transcended social circles. The key was to be genuine, supportive, and open-minded. He built a diverse network of friends who appreciated him for who he was and shared his values. This support system became his anchor, helping him navigate the ups and downs of middle school.

One afternoon, as Nathan sat in the cafeteria surrounded by friends from different groups, he realized how much he had grown. He no longer felt overwhelmed by the different social circles. Instead, he embraced the richness they brought to his life. By understanding, engaging, and balancing these relationships, Nathan had found his place in the vibrant tapestry of middle school.

Middle school was a journey of discovery, and Nathan learned that navigating social circles was about more than fitting in—it was about connecting, growing, and celebrating diversity. With this understanding, he felt confident and excited about the friendships and experiences that lay ahead.

As Nathan continued to navigate middle school, he found himself constantly balancing the desire to fit in with the need to stay true to himself. He observed how some students changed their personalities or interests just to be accepted by a particular group. Nathan didn't want to lose sight of who he was, and through trial and error, he developed a few key strategies for fitting in without compromising his identity.

MIDDLE SCHOOL TRIALS

One of the most important lessons Nathan learned was the value of authenticity. Pretending to be someone he wasn't just to gain acceptance felt exhausting and ultimately unfulfilling. He realized that true friends would appreciate him for who he truly was.

One day, during lunch, Nathan noticed a group of students discussing a popular video game. He had never played it and felt tempted to pretend he had, just to join the conversation. Instead, he decided to be honest. "I've never played that game, but it sounds interesting. What do you like about it?" he asked.

To his surprise, the group welcomed his curiosity and started explaining the game to him. They appreciated his honesty and openness, and Nathan learned something new. By being authentic, he was able to connect with others on a genuine level.

Finding common interests was another effective way for Nathan to fit in while staying true to himself. Instead of forcing himself into activities he didn't enjoy, he focused on shared passions that naturally brought people together.

Nathan loved nature and photography, so he joined the school's photography club. There, he met other students who shared his enthusiasm for capturing beautiful moments. They went on photo walks, shared tips, and showcased their work in school exhibitions. These activities allowed Nathan to bond with others over something he genuinely enjoyed, creating meaningful friendships in the process.

Middle school was filled with diverse personalities and backgrounds. Nathan learned that respecting differences was crucial for building strong, lasting relationships. He didn't have to agree with everyone's opinions or interests, but showing respect and empathy went a long way.

In his history class, group discussions often brought out varied perspectives. Nathan sometimes found himself in the minority opinion, but he chose to listen actively and respect his classmates' viewpoints. This approach not only helped him learn more but also earned him the respect of his peers. They appreciated his willingness to understand and his respectful demeanor, even when they disagreed.

Nathan understood the importance of setting boundaries. While he wanted to be social and make friends, he also needed time for himself and his own interests. It was okay to say no to things that didn't align with his values or made him uncomfortable.

One Friday, Ben invited Nathan to a party that sounded fun but conflicted with a commitment Nathan had made to help his dad with a project. Nathan felt torn but decided to honor his prior commitment. "Thanks for the invite, Ben, but I promised my dad I'd help him this weekend. Maybe next time?" he said.

Ben was understanding and respected Nathan's decision. By setting boundaries, Nathan maintained his integrity and balanced his personal and social life effectively.

Middle school often presented situations where Nathan's values were tested. He learned that staying true to his principles was crucial, even if it meant standing alone at times.

During a group project, some students suggested taking shortcuts that involved copying work from the internet. Nathan felt uncomfortable with the idea and voiced his concerns. "I think we should do the work ourselves. It's important to learn and be honest," he said.

Although his suggestion initially met with resistance, his group eventually agreed. They completed the project with integrity, and Nathan felt proud for standing by his values. His peers respected his

MIDDLE SCHOOL TRIALS

honesty and dedication, strengthening his friendships and his self-confidence.

While staying true to himself, Nathan also embraced the idea of trying new things. Being open to new experiences didn't mean changing who he was; it meant growing and learning in different ways.

When Mia invited him to audition for the school play, Nathan hesitated but decided to give it a shot. The experience pushed him out of his comfort zone and introduced him to a whole new circle of friends. He discovered a hidden talent for acting and gained confidence in his abilities.

Lastly, Nathan recognized the importance of surrounding himself with supportive friends who accepted him for who he was. He sought out friends who encouraged his individuality and shared his values.

Emily, Ben, Mia, and Lucas became his core group of friends. They supported each other through the ups and downs of middle school, celebrating successes and providing comfort during tough times. Their friendship was built on mutual respect, trust, and genuine connection.

Fitting in without losing oneself was a delicate balance, but Nathan discovered that it was entirely possible. By being authentic, finding common interests, respecting differences, setting boundaries, staying true to his values, being open to new experiences, and building a supportive network, he navigated middle school with confidence and integrity.

Nathan's journey taught him that fitting in didn't mean changing who he was. It meant finding the right people who valued and appreciated him for his true self. With these lessons in mind, he felt ready to face whatever challenges middle school had in store, secure in the knowledge that he could stay true to himself and thrive.

Middle school was a time of growth and discovery for Nathan, but it also came with the challenge of handling peer pressure. As he navigated new social circles and tried to fit in, Nathan encountered situations where his values and decisions were tested by the influence of others. Peer pressure often came in subtle forms. Sometimes, it was a direct challenge, and other times, it was an unspoken expectation. Nathan learned to recognize the signs of peer pressure, whether it was being urged to participate in an activity he wasn't comfortable with or feeling the need to conform to fit in.

One afternoon, Nathan was sitting with his friends Ben and a few of the soccer team members. They were talking about a big party happening that weekend at a popular student's house. Ben seemed particularly excited.

"Everyone's going to be there," Ben said. "You should come, Nathan. It'll be epic!"

Nathan hesitated. He had heard rumors that there might be alcohol at the party, and the idea made him uneasy. He didn't want to disappoint his friends, but he also didn't want to compromise his principles. Nathan realized that handling peer pressure required him to stand firm in his decisions. He thought about the values his parents had instilled in him and the importance of making choices that he felt comfortable with.

"Thanks for the invite, Ben," Nathan said, trying to sound confident. "But I don't think I'll go. I'm not really into big parties, especially if there's going to be drinking."

Ben raised an eyebrow but nodded. "I get it. Maybe next time."

Nathan felt a wave of relief wash over him. It wasn't easy to say no, but he knew he had made the right choice for himself. He appreciated Ben's understanding and felt a sense of pride for standing by his values.

MIDDLE SCHOOL TRIALS

Nathan also learned the importance of seeking support when dealing with peer pressure. He confided in his friend Emily about the party and his decision not to go.

"I'm glad you stuck to your guns," Emily said. "It's hard, but it's important to do what feels right for you. If you ever need someone to talk to or back you up, I'm here." Having supportive friends like Emily made a significant difference. Knowing that he wasn't alone in his decisions gave Nathan the strength to handle peer pressure more effectively.

Instead of isolating himself, Nathan found healthy alternatives to situations where peer pressure was strong. He discovered that he could still have fun and socialize without compromising his values. On the night of the party, Nathan and Emily planned a movie marathon at his house. They invited Lucas and Mia, and the four of them had a blast watching their favorite films, eating popcorn, and laughing together. It was a reminder that there were plenty of ways to enjoy middle school without giving in to peer pressure.

Nathan realized that being assertive was crucial when dealing with peer pressure. It wasn't just about saying no; it was about saying it confidently and respectfully.

During a lunch break, a group of students from Nathan's science class started talking about skipping the next class to hang out at the park. They turned to Nathan, expecting him to join.

"Come on, Nathan," one of them urged. "It'll be fun. Science is boring anyway."

Nathan felt the pressure building but remembered the importance of his education and responsibilities. "Thanks, but I can't skip class," he said firmly. "I want to keep up with my studies. Maybe we can all hang out after school instead?" His classmates were a bit disappointed, but they respected his decision. Nathan felt empowered by his ability to assert himself without alienating his peers.

There were times when Nathan gave in to peer pressure, but he learned valuable lessons from those experiences. One such incident happened during a group project when he agreed to use another student's work without proper credit. After the project was submitted, Nathan felt guilty and realized the importance of academic integrity. He decided to come clean to his teacher and apologized for his mistake. Miss. Martina appreciated his honesty and used the opportunity to discuss the importance of ethical behavior. Nathan's willingness to admit his mistake and learn from it reinforced his commitment to making better choices in the future. He understood that handling peer pressure was an ongoing process that required self-reflection and growth.

As Nathan continued to navigate middle school, he built self-confidence by trusting his instincts and making decisions that aligned with his values. He realized that fitting in didn't mean compromising who he was; it meant being confident in his choices and finding friends who respected him for them.

One day, as he walked down the hallway, he overheard a group of students talking about a prank they planned to pull on a teacher. They turned to Nathan, expecting him to join in.

"Are you in, Nathan?" one of them asked, a mischievous grin on his face. Nathan took a deep breath. "No, thanks. I don't think it's right to mess with teachers. I have too much respect for them."

The students shrugged and moved on, leaving Nathan feeling a mix of relief and pride. He had handled the peer pressure with confidence and integrity, reinforcing his commitment to staying true to himself.

Handling peer pressure was one of the biggest challenges Nathan faced in middle school, but it also became one of his greatest strengths.

MIDDLE SCHOOL TRIALS

By recognizing peer pressure, standing firm in his decisions, seeking support, finding alternatives, practicing assertiveness, learning from mistakes, and building self-confidence, Nathan navigated the complexities of middle school with integrity and resilience. Nathan learned that peer pressure was a natural part of growing up, but it didn't have to define his choices. With the right strategies and support, he found a balance between fitting in and staying true to himself, ready to face whatever challenges lay ahead in his middle school journey.

Chapter 3: Surviving the Cafeteria

The school cafeteria can be a daunting place for any middle school student, and Nathan was no exception. The first day he walked into the cafeteria, the sheer noise and bustle were overwhelming. Students clustered in tight groups at tables, talking and laughing, while others moved quickly through the lunch line. Nathan felt a knot of anxiety tighten in his stomach as he scanned the room, searching for a place to sit. He clutched his lunch tray and took a deep breath. He remembered his mom's advice that morning: "Just be yourself, and you'll find your place." But at that moment, being himself seemed incredibly difficult. The cafeteria was a sea of faces, most of which he didn't know well.

He spotted a table where a few students from his homeroom class were sitting. They seemed friendly enough, so he decided to give it a try. As he approached, he noticed Emily waving at him. Relieved, Nathan made his way over and asked, "Mind if I join you?"

"Of course not!" Emily replied with a smile. "We were just talking about the science project. How's yours coming along?" Nathan relaxed a little as he took a seat. The conversation flowed easily, and he was grateful for Emily's welcoming presence. It wasn't as scary as he had imagined.

Over the next few weeks, Nathan decided to explore sitting with different groups to find where he felt most comfortable. This exploration helped him learn more about his classmates and their interests.

One day, he sat with Lucas and his friends from the art club. They were discussing their latest projects and upcoming art shows. Nathan, who enjoyed photography, found himself intrigued by their conversations. Lucas even invited him to join their after-school sketching sessions.

Another day, Nathan joined Ben and the soccer team. The table was lively, filled with jokes and sports banter. Nathan wasn't the most athletic, but he enjoyed the camaraderie and enthusiasm of the athletes. Then, he spent a few lunches with Mia and the drama club members. Their table was always animated, with discussions about plays, rehearsals, and acting techniques. Nathan found their passion for theater infectious, and he enjoyed their creative energy.

While Nathan enjoyed exploring different groups, he realized that he needed to find a consistent place where he could feel at home. He noticed that the cafeteria had a few quieter corners where smaller groups gathered. One day, he saw a group of students who seemed a bit like him—friendly but not particularly tied to any specific clique.

He approached them, recognizing a few faces from his science and math classes. "Hey, is this seat taken?" he asked. One of the students, Sarah, smiled and shook her head. "Nope, feel free to join us. We're just talking about the new Marvel movie."

Nathan felt an instant connection. He loved Marvel movies and found himself easily joining the conversation. Over the next few days, he continued to sit with this group. They were diverse in their interests but shared a common ground in their mutual respect and open-mindedness. He also found that sitting with this new group allowed him to be himself without pressure. They were welcoming and inclusive, and he started to look forward to lunch breaks. He realized that sometimes, finding the right place to sit was less about fitting into a specific group and more about finding people who accepted him for who he was.

One day, as they were eating lunch, Sarah asked, "Hey Nathan, we're planning to go to the arcade this weekend. Want to come?" "Sure!" Nathan replied, feeling excited. He realized that these were the kind of friends he had been looking for—people who shared his interests and valued his company.

Of course, not every day in the cafeteria was perfect. There were times when Nathan felt awkward or out of place, and there were days when finding a seat was a challenge. But he learned to handle these situations with resilience. If he ever felt uncomfortable, he reminded himself that it was okay to move to another table or even sit alone for a while. It wasn't a reflection of his worth or likability. On tougher days, he focused on enjoying his meal and planning his next steps.

Surviving the cafeteria was one of the many challenges Nathan faced in middle school, but it also became an opportunity for growth and connection. By exploring different groups, being open and friendly, and staying true to himself, Nathan found a place where he belonged. The cafeteria, once an intimidating space, became a place of friendship and laughter, marking another step in his journey through middle school.

Chapter 4: Cafeteria Chronicles and Canteen Chaos

Nathan's middle school cafeteria was legendary. Not for its gourmet meals, mind you, but for the dubious quality of its food. The canteen, on the other hand, was a haven of junk food, a refuge for those seeking solace from the cafeteria's questionable cuisine.

Nathan's first encounter with the school cafeteria was an eye-opener. The menu boasted a variety of items that seemed relatively harmless at first glance: pizza, spaghetti, mystery meatloaf. But the reality was a different story.

"Nathan, have you ever seen pizza that looks like a frisbee?" Zack asked one day, holding up a slice that wobbled ominously.

"I think it's supposed to be pepperoni, but I'm not sure those red circles are actually edible," Nathan replied, eyeing the pizza with suspicion.

The spaghetti was another adventure. The sauce was a peculiar shade of orange, resembling more of a science experiment gone wrong than a marinara sauce. The noodles were either mushy to the point of disintegration or as chewy as rubber bands. Nathan had once tried to twirl a forkful, only to have it snap back and hit him in the face.

"Nice spaghetti slingshot," Gabe had said, barely containing his laughter.

And then there was the infamous mystery meatloaf. No one knew exactly what it was made of, and rumors abounded. Some said it was a mix of leftover meats from the previous week. Others believed it contained vegetables so finely diced that they had become invisible.

"Whatever you do, don't ask what's in it," advised a seasoned eighth-grader. "Ignorance is bliss."

Nathan took the advice to heart, but that didn't stop him from occasionally poking at the meatloaf with a fork, half-expecting it to poke back.

Fortunately, there was the canteen, a beacon of hope amidst the culinary disasters. Stocked with an array of junk food, it was the place where students could indulge their taste buds without fear.

The canteen sold everything from chips and candy bars to sugary sodas and neon-colored slushies. Nathan and his friends would often pool their spare change to buy a feast of snack foods that, while nutritionally questionable, were infinitely more appealing than cafeteria offerings.

"Guys, look what I got!" Nathan exclaimed one afternoon, triumphantly holding up a bag of Flamin' Hot Cheetos and a can of Mountain Dew.

"Awesome! We can have our own mini party," Zack said, grabbing a pack of gummy worms.

They'd sit on the benches outside, munching away on their junk food bounty, laughing and joking about the latest cafeteria mishap.

"Do you think they actually test the food in the cafeteria?" Gabe wondered aloud, biting into a chocolate bar.

"If they do, they must have taste testers with no taste buds," Nathan quipped, eliciting a round of laughter.

The cafeteria became a source of endless entertainment. There was the time when the Jell-O was so jiggly that it bounced off plates and onto the floor, leading to an impromptu game of Jell-O dodgeball. And who could forget the day when the mashed potatoes were so sticky that they could be used as glue? Nathan had accidentally glued his spoon to his tray and had to ask for help prying it loose.

In contrast, the canteen adventures were a treat. The thrill of choosing from a rainbow of sugary options was the highlight of many school days. The canteen staff, always friendly, would often chuckle at the students' excitement.

"Back again for more candy, Nathan?" the canteen lady would say with a knowing smile.

"You bet! Need something to wash down that cafeteria lunch," Nathan would reply with a wink.

As the school year progressed, the contrast between the cafeteria and the canteen became a running joke. Nathan and his friends even staged a mock debate: "Cafeteria Food vs. Canteen Snacks."

"Ladies and gentlemen," Nathan began, standing on a bench in the schoolyard, "I present to you Exhibit A: cafeteria pizza, which can double as a frisbee or a very effective doorstop."

"Exhibit B," Zack chimed in, holding up a bag of potato chips, "canteen snacks that are delicious, crunchy, and unlikely to bounce off your plate."

The "debate" ended with everyone unanimously declaring the canteen the winner. They celebrated with a feast of junk food, toasting with their slushies and cheering their victory over cafeteria cuisine.

As Nathan looked back on his middle school years, he realized that the cafeteria catastrophes and canteen adventures had been an integral part of his experience. They had provided endless laughs, unforgettable moments, and a unique bond with his friends.

Sure, the cafeteria food was often a mystery best left unsolved, but it had also been the backdrop for some of the funniest and most memorable times of his middle school life. And the canteen, with its shelves of junk food, had been a sweet refuge in the chaos.

Nathan knew that as he moved on to high school, he would carry these culinary memories with him, forever grateful for the laughter and camaraderie they had brought. And who knew? Maybe the high school cafeteria would have its own set of surprises and adventures waiting to be discovered.

Chapter 5: The Homework Nightmare

Middle school brought a significant increase in homework for Nathan. Balancing multiple subjects, projects, and extracurricular activities felt overwhelming. The first few weeks were especially tough, and Nathan quickly found himself in what he called "the homework nightmare." But through this struggle, he learned effective study habits that made his life easier and his learning more enjoyable.

One Thursday evening, Nathan sat at his desk staring at the mountain of textbooks, worksheets, and project outlines spread before him. He had math problems to solve, a history essay to write, and a science project due next week. The sheer volume of work made his head spin.

"I don't even know where to start," Nathan muttered to himself. He grabbed his phone and sent a quick message to Emily. *Do you have a ton of homework too? How do you manage all this?*

Emily replied almost instantly. *Yeah, it's a lot. I usually break it down into smaller tasks. Want me to show you how I do it?*

The next day, Nathan and Emily met in the library after school. Emily pulled out her planner and a notebook. "The first thing I do is write down all my assignments," she said. "Then, I break them down into smaller, more manageable tasks."

Nathan watched as Emily divided her homework into smaller parts. Instead of seeing "write history essay," she had tasks like "research topic," "write outline," and "draft introduction."

"Wow, that looks so much less intimidating," Nathan said, feeling a bit more hopeful.

Emily also showed Nathan how to create a study schedule. "It's important to plan your time," she explained. "I usually study in chunks of time and take breaks in between."

Nathan decided to give it a try. That evening, he wrote down all his tasks and created a schedule. He planned to start with math for 30 minutes, take a 10-minute break, then work on his history essay for another 30 minutes. He left time for dinner and a short review session before bed.

Nathan realized that staying organized was crucial. He designated a specific place for his school supplies and used different folders for each subject. This way, he didn't waste time searching for materials.

He also started using a planner to keep track of assignments, tests, and due dates. Checking off completed tasks gave him a sense of accomplishment and kept him motivated.

Nathan discovered that he didn't have to tackle everything alone. He began to utilize resources available to him. He visited the school library to find books and articles for his history essay, and he watched educational videos to help with his science project.

He also joined a study group with Ben, Lucas, and a few other classmates. They met twice a week to review material, discuss difficult topics, and quiz each other. Working with peers not only made studying more effective but also more enjoyable.

One of the most important lessons Nathan learned was the importance of asking for help. Initially, he felt embarrassed to admit when he didn't understand something. But as the workload increased, he realized that seeking help was essential.

MIDDLE SCHOOL TRIALS

Nathan started asking questions in class and visiting teachers during office hours. He found that his teachers were more than willing to provide extra explanations and guidance. For math, he even attended a few after-school tutoring sessions, which made a huge difference in his understanding.

Time management became a crucial skill for Nathan. He learned to prioritize tasks based on their deadlines and difficulty levels. He tackled the hardest assignments first when his energy and concentration levels were highest.

Nathan also started setting specific goals for each study session. Instead of vaguely planning to "study math," he aimed to "complete five math problems." This approach made his study sessions more focused and productive.

Nathan realized that maintaining a healthy lifestyle was essential for effective studying. He made sure to get enough sleep, eat nutritious meals, and stay active. Regular exercise, like playing soccer or going for a run, helped him relieve stress and stay energized.

He also incorporated short breaks into his study sessions to avoid burnout. During these breaks, he would stretch, grab a snack, or simply relax for a few minutes before getting back to work.

Procrastination was a habit Nathan struggled with. He often found himself putting off tasks until the last minute, leading to late-night study sessions and stress. To combat this, he started using the "two-minute rule": if a task could be done in two minutes or less, he did it immediately. This helped him tackle small tasks quickly and avoid them piling up.

Nathan also set specific deadlines for himself, even if they were earlier than the actual due dates. This gave him a buffer period to review and refine his work, reducing last-minute panic.

Over time, Nathan regularly reflected on his study habits and made adjustments as needed. He noted what worked well and what didn't. For instance, he realized that he focused better in the library than at home, where distractions were plentiful. He also found that studying with a friend could be both productive and motivating.

As Nathan implemented these effective study habits, he noticed a significant improvement in his schoolwork. His grades improved, and he felt more confident in his abilities. The overwhelming stress of the "homework nightmare" began to fade, replaced by a sense of control and accomplishment.

One evening, as Nathan finished his homework ahead of schedule, he smiled with satisfaction. He had come a long way from the overwhelmed student he had been at the start of the school year. By developing and sticking to effective study habits, Nathan transformed his approach to homework and learning, paving the way for continued success in middle school and beyond.

Nathan's journey from the chaos of the homework nightmare to mastering effective study habits was a testament to his resilience and willingness to learn. By breaking down tasks, creating a study schedule, staying organized, using resources, asking for help, managing time, maintaining a healthy lifestyle, overcoming procrastination, and reflecting on his habits, Nathan turned his academic challenges into triumphs.

Middle school continued to present new challenges, but with the study habits he had developed, Nathan felt equipped to handle them with confidence and efficiency.

Middle school wasn't just about classes for Nathan—it was a circus of balancing schoolwork with a flurry of extracurricular activities that sometimes felt like juggling flaming bowling pins. As if navigating

MIDDLE SCHOOL TRIALS

algebra wasn't challenging enough, Nathan found himself signed up for a mix of activities that made his schedule resemble a Rubik's Cube on overdrive. Monday afternoons were dedicated to soccer practice, where Coach Davis's booming voice echoed like a motivational soundtrack. "Come on, team! Hustle harder than you hustle for pizza!"

Tuesdays meant art club, where Miss. Rina, with her vibrant hair and penchant for abstract expressionism, guided them through painting sessions that often ended with more paint on Nathan's face than on the canvas.

Wednesdays saw Nathan grappling with the intricacies of drama club, where Mr. Sam, in his dramatic flair, insisted on their best Shakespearean accents. "To be, or not to be—get it right, Nathan, or the ghost of Hamlet's father will haunt you!" Thursdays were the science experiment extravaganza. Nathan, armed with safety goggles and a lab coat three sizes too big (thanks to a mix-up with the school supply order), embarked on chemistry experiments that sometimes resulted in explosions that left the classroom smelling like a failed barbecue. Fridays, however, were reserved for the melodic chaos of band practice. Nathan, attempting to master the trumpet, often hit notes that made nearby dogs howl in sympathy. Mr. Alan's determined smile reassured him, "Practice makes perfect, Nathan! Or at least, less likely to alarm the neighborhood."

But amid this whirlwind of activities, Nathan faced a daunting reality: homework. It lurked like a lurking thing, waiting to ambush his free time with algebra problems, history essays, and science reports that seemed longer than a marathon.

Finding time for homework was an adventure in itself. Some nights, Nathan tried to multitask by balancing a textbook on his knee during soccer drills. Coach Davis raised an eyebrow. "Nathan, are you analyzing the physics of goal kicks or practicing your trigonometry?"

Other times, he attempted to sneak in a few history readings during art club, only to end up with sketches of historical figures in Renaissance attire.

Sleep became a rare treasure, coveted like a mythical creature. With rehearsals, practices, and late-night study sessions, Nathan often found himself resembling a sleep-deprived zombie during morning classes. Mr. Mark, the history teacher, once mistook Nathan's yawn for a dramatic reenactment of the Battle of Hastings.

Through the chaos and occasional mishaps, Nathan learned valuable lessons. He discovered that time management wasn't just a phrase teachers repeated—it was a survival skill. Planning became his superpower, scheduling study sessions between trumpet blasts and soccer drills. He also learned the art of improvisation—whether it was crafting a last-minute history essay using soccer analogies or applying drama club theatrics to science presentations. As Nathan juggled his way through middle school, he found moments of joy amidst the chaos. Band performances where the notes finally aligned, art club exhibitions where his splattered canvases were met with applause, and soccer victories that felt like conquering the world. In the end, balancing schoolwork and extracurricular activities wasn't just about surviving—it was about thriving in the whirlwind of middle school life. Nathan, with paint-stained hands and a backpack full of textbooks, emerged not just as a student but as a master juggler of academics and adventures.

And so, the middle school circus continued, with Nathan at its center ring. Through laughter, mishaps, and the occasional trumpet blast, he navigated the balancing act of schoolwork and extracurricular extravagance, ready for whatever twists and turns the next act would bring. After all, as Coach Davis would say, "Life's a game of soccer—kick hard, aim high, and don't forget your homework!"

Chapter 6: Dealing with Bullies

Middle school wasn't just about textbooks and awkward locker combinations for Nathan—it was a crash course in dealing with bullies. From the moment Brad, the self-proclaimed dodgeball king, decided Nathan's glasses made him an easy target, Nathan knew he was in for a wild ride.

"Nice goggles, four-eyes!" Brad would jeer, sending the cafeteria into fits of laughter. Nathan, not exactly blessed with a quick comeback gene, often found himself staring blankly, wondering if there was a comeback manual hidden in the library somewhere.

But Nathan wasn't one to let the insults get the best of him for long. Armed with a mix of wit (borrowed from some sitcoms) and sheer stubbornness (thanks, Mom), he decided to turn the tables.

"Hey, Brad," Nathan quipped one day, "if I didn't have these glasses, I might mistake you for someone who cares."

The lunchroom froze for a moment, then erupted in laughter—even Brad had to crack a smile. Nathan realized that sometimes, a well-timed joke could be more powerful than any dodgeball victory.

Of course, not every bully was as easily disarmed. There were times when Nathan had to rely on his friends and trusted adults. From talking it out with teachers (who seemed to have a sixth sense for cafeteria drama) to sharing his woes with his endlessly supportive parents (who once offered to bring in their old '80s dance moves to scare off any bullies), Nathan learned that facing bullies wasn't just about standing up for himself—it was about finding humor in the chaos and building a community of support.

Miss Erin was the no-nonsense middle school coordinator who could make the toughest bully retreat faster than you could say "detention slip." With a gaze that could freeze lava and a voice that could quiet a tornado, she ruled the school corridors with unwavering authority. Bullies learned quickly that messing with Miss. Erin meant facing consequences that were as swift as they were effective.

Her office was a beacon of order amidst the chaos of middle school drama, adorned with posters declaring, "Bullying Stops Here!" and "Kindness Counts!" Miss Erin had a knack for sniffing out trouble before it escalated, and her no-nonsense approach to discipline left no room for excuses.

Rumor had it that when a group of troublemakers dared to prank her office with rubber chickens and whoopee cushions, Miss Erin turned the tables by orchestrating an impromptu talent show where the pranksters had to showcase their "skills" to the entire school. It was a lesson in humility that left them not only regretting their antics but also marveling at Miss Erin's creative retribution.

Under Miss Erin's watchful eye, the middle school became a sanctuary where bullies faced not only consequences but also opportunities for growth and reflection. Her commitment to creating a safe and respectful environment earned her respect from students and admiration from colleagues, making her a true champion against bullying in the middle school trenches.

Head Teacher Mr. Allen was not just a leader in name but a formidable force against bullying at Nathan's school. With a towering presence matched only by his ability to appear out of nowhere (like a ninja principal), he made it clear that bullying had no place in his halls. Rumor had it that he once turned a group of hallway tormentors into a impromptu choir for a surprise performance at a PTA meeting—a lesson in harmony they wouldn't soon forget. His office door was

MIDDLE SCHOOL TRIALS

adorned with a sign that read, "Bullies beware: I speak softly and carry a big detention slip." Despite his stern demeanor, Head Teacher Allen's knack for defusing tension with a well-timed dad joke or an unexpected dance move earned him both respect and occasional giggles from even the most hardened troublemakers.

Head Teacher Allen wasn't alone in his quest to stamp out bullying at Nathan's school. Teacher Jojo, known affectionately as "The Name Whisperer," had a unique superpower: he knew every student in the entire school by name and could spot a potential bully from across the playground. His ability to diffuse conflicts with a simple, "Now, now, let's all take a deep breath and remember we're here to learn and grow," was legendary among students and staff alike.

When Teacher Jojo sensed bullying brewing, he didn't hesitate to intervene. His gentle but firm approach included one-on-one talks with both the victim and the aggressor, helping them understand the impact of their actions. Rumor had it that he once thwarted a lunchroom skirmish by challenging the bullies to a spontaneous spelling bee—where the correct spelling of "respect" proved more daunting than any physical altercation.

Together, Head Teacher Allen's authoritative presence and Teacher Jojo's empathetic guidance created a school environment where kindness and respect were not just encouraged but enforced. Their tag-team approach to bullying not only kept the halls safe but also fostered a sense of community where every student felt seen, heard, and valued.

Looking back on those middle school battles, Nathan realized they weren't just challenges—they were character-building exercises disguised as lunchroom drama. And through it all, he emerged with a knack for handling life's curveballs and a sense of humor that could defuse even the most awkward of situations. Middle school might have been a battlefield of bullies, but Nathan, armed with wit and resilience, conquered it one sarcastic quip at a time.

Chapter 7: Taming Teacher Troubles

Middle school wasn't just about dodging dodgeballs for Nathan—it was navigating the minefield of teacher personalities. From the algebra-loving Ms. Smith to the history buff Mr. Mark, each teacher brought their own quirks and challenges. Nathan quickly learned that building positive relationships with teachers wasn't just a good idea—it was a survival strategy.

First up was Ms. Algebra, whose love for numbers rivaled Nathan's passion for video games. Her daily math puzzles could make even the savviest Sudoku enthusiast break a sweat. Nathan, armed with a notebook filled with doodles of dragons and secret ninja codes, soon found himself at odds with her strict "show your work" policy. "Come on, Nathan," Ms. Algebra would exclaim, peering over her glasses, "math is like solving mysteries—you can't just summon answers from the void!"

Undeterred, Nathan tried to charm his way into her good graces with a math-themed joke: "Why was the equal sign so humble? Because he knew he wasn't less than or greater than anyone else!" Ms. Algebra's stern facade cracked just a bit, and Nathan earned himself a half-smile and a nod of approval.

Next on Nathan's hit list was Mr. Mark, the self-proclaimed history buff with a penchant for dramatic retellings of ancient battles. Nathan, more interested in the latest gaming updates than the Battle of Hastings, found himself nodding along while mentally calculating the odds of finding a hidden treasure in the school cafeteria.

"Imagine, Nathan," Mr. Mark would declare, sweeping his arms dramatically, "if we could travel back in time to witness the fall of

Rome!" Nathan, ever the quick thinker, piped up, "Or we could just ask Principal Allen—he seems to have been around since the Stone Age!" The class erupted in laughter, including Mr. Mark, who couldn't help but appreciate Nathan's wit, even if it was at his expense.

As Nathan navigated through the maze of teacher troubles, he discovered that sometimes the key to winning them over was in unexpected places. He tackled Ms. Smith's algebra challenges with newfound determination, even offering to tutor classmates who were as lost as he initially was. He approached Mr. Mark's history assignments with a creative twist, turning a project on ancient civilizations into a Minecraft-inspired virtual tour of the pyramids.

Slowly but surely, Nathan's efforts paid off. Ms. Algebra softened her stance on doodles in notebooks, admitting that creativity and problem-solving often went hand in hand. Mr. Mark appreciated Nathan's unique perspective on history, even incorporating his gaming analogies into lessons to keep the class engaged. As Nathan reflected on his journey through teacher troubles, he realized that middle school wasn't just about surviving—it was about thriving amidst the chaos and building bridges with humor and determination. By navigating algebraic mysteries, unraveling historical dramas, and embracing each teacher's quirks with a touch of middle school humor, Nathan forged positive relationships that not only helped him succeed academically but also made the journey a lot more fun.

Middle school might have been a battleground of teacher troubles, but Nathan, armed with quick wit and a willingness to learn, emerged victorious, ready to face high school with a smile and a knack for turning classroom challenges into comedy gold.

Middle school wasn't all fun and games for Nathan; there were the occasional dragons in the form of difficult or unfair teachers to slay. From the dragon lady who graded essays with a red pen that seemed to

MIDDLE SCHOOL TRIALS

bleed more than correct, to the wizard of algebra who could summon the most perplexing equations at will, Nathan faced his fair share of academic challenges.

First on Nathan's list was Ms. Grimsby, the English teacher with a reputation for wielding her red pen like a weapon of mass destruction. Her essays came back looking like they'd been through a battlefield, covered in more red ink than a spilled potion in a wizard's laboratory.

Undeterred by the sea of corrections, Nathan devised a plan. Armed with a thesaurus and a penchant for elaborate metaphors, he decided to turn his next essay into a literary masterpiece. "My essay," he declared dramatically, "is a phoenix rising from the ashes of misplaced commas and run-on sentences!"

Ms. Grimsby, despite her stern demeanor, couldn't help but appreciate Nathan's flair for the dramatic. She rewarded him with a slightly less red-marked paper and a begrudging nod of approval.

Next was Ms. Smith's, the algebra wizard whose equations seemed more like ancient runes than simple math problems. Nathan, armed with a pencil and a determination fueled by caffeine-free soda, tackled each problem like a knight facing a fire-breathing dragon.

When confronted with an impossible equation that threatened to unravel the fabric of reality, Nathan resorted to a tactic passed down from generations of math-averse heroes: drawing doodles of perplexed dragons in the margins. "Even dragons," he reasoned, "struggle with the concept of imaginary numbers!"

Ms. Smith's, who had seen his fair share of math escapades, couldn't help but chuckle at Nathan's doodles. He offered some extra tutoring sessions and a more manageable approach to tackling algebraic mysteries, which Nathan gladly accepted.

ROSEANNE GODKIN

As Nathan navigated the realm of unfair teachers, he discovered that sometimes the best weapon against academic dragons was a blend of diplomacy and doodles. He learned to advocate for himself with a mix of charm and creativity, turning seemingly impossible tasks into opportunities for comedic relief.

By the end of the school year, Nathan had not only conquered the challenges posed by difficult teachers but had also forged unexpected alliances through humor and perseverance. Ms. Grimsby's red pen became less daunting, and Ms. Smith's algebraic sorcery felt more like a puzzle than a curse.

As Nathan reflected on his battles with unfair teachers, he realized that middle school wasn't just about surviving—it was about finding humor in the most challenging of situations and turning academic struggles into triumphs. Armed with quick wit, a touch of creativity, and a willingness to learn, Nathan emerged victorious, ready to face the next academic adventure with a grin and a pencil sharpened for whatever dragons might come his way. Middle school might have been a realm of academic dragons, but Nathan, armed with humor and determination, proved that even the fiercest challenges could be conquered with a well-timed joke and a doodle or two.

Parent-teacher conferences were a biannual event that struck fear into the hearts of middle schoolers everywhere—including Nathan. Facing his parents and teachers in the same room felt like navigating a maze with hidden traps and pitfalls. Each term, Nathan braced himself for the inevitable: the good, the bad, and the occasionally cringe-worthy.

Before the conferences, Nathan embarked on a reconnaissance mission worthy of a secret agent. Armed with a backpack full of graded assignments (the good, the bad, and the borderline embarrassing), he pored over each grade and comment like a detective unraveling a mystery.

MIDDLE SCHOOL TRIALS

"Ah, Ms. Algebra's raised eyebrow at my latest test score—definitely a code red," Nathan muttered to himself, scribbling down potential excuses and promises to improve.

First up was Ms. Grimsby, whose red pen had left more marks on Nathan's essays than a swarm of disgruntled bees. As she explained the finer points of essay structure to his parents, Nathan silently prayed that his metaphors had impressed her enough to soften the sting of criticism.

"Your son," Ms. Grimsby began, her red pen poised like a sword, "shows potential but needs to focus more on clarity and less on dramatic flair." Nathan nodded solemnly, secretly vowing to retire his phoenix metaphors—at least until high school.

Next was Ms. Smith, the algebra wizard whose equations had Nathan questioning the existence of integers altogether. Nathan's strategy here was simple: deflect with charm and distract with doodles of perplexed dragons.

"Ah, Ms. Smith," Nathan's dad chuckled, eyeing the equations on display, "I see Nathan's penchant for creativity extends to his mathematical approach." Ms. Smith, ever the enigmatic wizard, nodded thoughtfully, offering pointers on Nathan's progress and a promise of extra tutoring sessions—which Nathan accepted with all the grace of a knight offered an extra shield before battle.

Despite the anxiety, Nathan discovered that parent-teacher conferences weren't just about surviving—they were about finding common ground and mutual understanding. He learned to navigate the delicate balance between parental expectations and teacher feedback, sometimes with a well-timed joke or a strategic nod of agreement.

By the end of each conference, Nathan emerged with a newfound sense of purpose and a clearer path forward. He realized that facing academic challenges head-on, with humor and humility, was the key to turning dreaded conferences into opportunities for growth and collaboration. As Nathan reflected on his journey through parent-teacher conferences, he realized that middle school wasn't just about grades—it was about building bridges between home and school, and finding humor in the most nerve-wracking of situations. Armed with newfound insights and a backpack lighter by a few graded assignments, Nathan faced each term with renewed confidence, ready to tackle academic adventures and parent-teacher dialogues alike with a grin and a plan for success.

Middle school might have been a maze of parent-teacher conferences, but Nathan, armed with resilience and a touch of middle school charm, navigated each term like a seasoned explorer, discovering that even the most dreaded events could lead to moments of understanding and growth.

Chapter 8: Detentions

Middle school wasn't all fun and games for Nathan. Alongside the friendships and laughter, there were also the inevitable detentions and not-so-great moments that came with navigating the tricky landscape of adolescence. Nathan learned the hard way that middle school was a place where mistakes were made, lessons were learned, and character was built, often through experiences that were far from enjoyable.

Nathan's first brush with detention came as a shock. It all started with a harmless prank involving an overstuffed locker and a carefully balanced stack of textbooks. The plan was simple: give his friend Zack a mild scare when he opened his locker. What Nathan didn't anticipate was the chain reaction that followed, causing a hallway disruption of epic proportions.

"Nathan Moore, report to the principal's office immediately," blared the announcement over the intercom. Nathan's stomach dropped as he trudged to the office, the walk feeling like a march to his doom.

Principal Allen, known for his strict yet fair demeanor, greeted Nathan with a stern look. "Care to explain why you thought turning the hallway into an obstacle course was a good idea?"

Nathan's attempt at humor—"I was just trying to help Zack with his organizational skills"—fell flat. Detention it was.

Detention wasn't quite the horror show Nathan imagined, but it wasn't a picnic either. Sitting in a silent room with other offenders, Nathan quickly realized that staring at the clock didn't make time move faster.

He tried to make the best of it, doodling in the margins of his notebook and mentally composing an apology to Zack, who thankfully found the prank more amusing than annoying. The real challenge, though, was facing his parents.

"Nathan, we're disappointed," his mom said, her usual warm smile replaced with a frown. "Detention isn't a joke. You need to take responsibility for your actions."

His dad nodded in agreement. "It's not about the prank, it's about disrupting others and not thinking through the consequences. We expect better from you."

Navigating social circles was another challenge. There were moments when Nathan felt left out or misunderstood, and dealing with cliques sometimes felt like negotiating peace treaties between rival nations. There were days when the cafeteria felt like a battlefield and days when the weight of schoolwork felt like too much to bear.

Despite the rough patches, Nathan learned valuable lessons from his not-so-good experiences. Detention taught him the importance of thinking before acting and considering the impact of his actions on others. Dealing with the less pleasant aspects of middle school life helped him develop resilience and empathy.

"I guess middle school isn't just about surviving," Nathan mused to his friend Gabe one afternoon. "It's about learning from the bumps and bruises along the way."

Gabe, ever the optimist, nodded. "Yeah, and at least we've got each other to get through it. Plus, imagine the stories we'll have to tell when we're older!"

Nathan realized that the not-so-good parts of middle school were just as important as the good times. They shaped his character, taught him

MIDDLE SCHOOL TRIALS

responsibility, and helped him appreciate the support of his friends and family. Embracing both the highs and lows, Nathan faced each day with a mix of determination and humor, knowing that every experience, good or bad, was a step towards growing up.

Middle school was a wild ride, full of unexpected detours and valuable lessons. As Nathan looked forward to high school, he carried with him the knowledge that even the toughest moments could be transformed into opportunities for growth and laughter.

Chapter 9: Extracurricular Adventures

Middle school wasn't just about surviving classes and dodging cafeteria chaos for Nathan—it was also a chance to stumble upon unexpected passions through extracurricular activities. From finding his niche to mastering the art of juggling schoolwork and hobbies, Nathan embarked on a journey of discovery that would shape his middle school experience in hilarious and unpredictable ways.

Nathan's quest for the perfect extracurricular activity began with a trial-and-error approach that would impress even the bravest of adventurers. He tried everything from the debate club, where arguments were more intense than lunchroom debates over the best pizza topping, to the school newspaper, where he discovered a knack for uncovering breaking news like the mystery of who stole the principal's beloved rubber chicken.

"Maybe chess will sharpen my strategic thinking," Nathan mused, contemplating his next move against a wily opponent who seemed to have memorized every move in the knight's playbook. Despite a few embarrassing losses where his pawn somehow ended up moonwalking across the board, Nathan persisted, finding joy in the mental gymnastics of each match.

Yet it was on the soccer field where Nathan found his true calling. With cleats laced and determination etched on his face, he discovered a passion for teamwork and the thrill of scoring that made every practice feel like a mini World Cup final. Even when he accidentally kicked the ball into the wrong goal during his first game, Nathan's team rallied behind him with encouragement that echoed louder than the coach's halftime speeches.

MIDDLE SCHOOL TRIALS

With soccer added to his weekly schedule, Nathan faced the challenge of balancing practice drills with algebra equations and history essays. It was a delicate dance between dribbling drills and study sessions, but Nathan quickly learned the art of time management worthy of a multitasking wizard.

"Maybe I can sneak in some algebra practice during halftime," Nathan joked with his coach, who raised an eyebrow but appreciated the dedication. Nathan became a master of cramming for tests during bus rides to away games and squeezing in homework between soccer drills, occasionally mistaking his math notes for soccer strategies and drawing soccer plays on his algebra homework.

Through trial, error, and the occasional last-minute cram session, Nathan discovered that balancing school and hobbies wasn't just about managing time—it was about prioritizing passions and finding joy in the journey. He also learned that running laps around the field was great for clearing his mind after a particularly tough geometry problem.

As Nathan immersed himself deeper into soccer and school clubs, he discovered a treasure trove of benefits beyond just honing skills. Joining clubs and teams not only strengthened his social circle but also boosted his confidence and leadership skills. "Who knew," Nathan marveled, scoring a decisive goal in a tense match, "that being captain of the chess club could prepare me for rallying my teammates on the field?" His chess club teammates nodded enthusiastically, having witnessed Nathan's ability to strategize moves on and off the board.

From forging friendships with teammates who shared his love for the game to learning to collaborate with peers in coding club projects, Nathan realized that extracurricular activities were more than just hobbies—they were pathways to personal growth and memorable middle school adventures. He also discovered that coding robots sometimes resulted in dance parties when the robots decided to break into spontaneous disco moves.

As Nathan reflected on his extracurricular adventures, he realized that middle school was a place where passions were discovered, skills were sharpened, and friendships were forged on and off the field. Whether kicking goals on the soccer field or strategizing chess moves in the club room, Nathan embraced each activity with enthusiasm and a determination to make the most of his middle school years.

Armed with newfound skills in time management, teamwork, and the art of balancing priorities (and occasionally still mixing up his soccer playbook with his science notes), Nathan faced each day with a sense of purpose and excitement. Middle school wasn't just about surviving—it was about thriving through extracurricular adventures that shaped him into a well-rounded student and teammate, ready to tackle the next challenge with a grin and a soccer ball at his feet. And maybe, just maybe, he'd find a way to incorporate his love for soccer into his next science project—robotic goalie, anyone?

Chapter 10: The Rich Tapestry of School Life

Nathan's middle school experience wouldn't have been complete without the excitement of school games, cultural days, and a variety of other non-academic activities. These events were a chance to showcase talents, learn about different cultures, and bond with classmates in ways that were impossible in a traditional classroom setting.

The highlight of the year for Nathan and his friends was always the friendly school games. These competitions, held both at their school and away at other schools, were a mix of sports, camaraderie, and good-natured rivalry.

Nathan was part of the school's soccer team, and their first away game of the season was against Kenton Middle School. The team piled onto the bus, buzzing with anticipation and a bit of nervousness.

"Alright, team, remember our strategy: pass the ball, keep moving, and try not to trip over your own feet," Coach Davis said, giving Zack a pointed look, which made everyone laugh.

The game was intense. Nathan found himself sprinting down the field, dodging defenders, and trying to keep his breath steady. Zack managed to score a goal, much to everyone's surprise, and Nathan couldn't help but laugh as Zack celebrated like he'd just won the World Cup.

In the end, their team won 3-2, and the bus ride back was filled with cheers and impromptu karaoke sessions, much to the driver's chagrin.

Cultural Days were a favorite at Nathan's school. Each class would represent a different country, and students would dress in traditional attire, prepare foods from that culture, and give presentations about their chosen nation. Nathan's class had been assigned Japan one year, and they went all out. The classroom was decorated with paper lanterns, cherry blossom branches, and posters of famous landmarks. Nathan wore a kimono, which he found surprisingly comfortable, and helped prepare sushi rolls and mochi for the food stall.

During the presentations, Gabe, who had a knack for languages, attempted to teach the class a few basic Japanese phrases. It was going well until he accidentally said something that had the teacher blushing and the students in stitches.

"That's definitely not how you say 'good morning,'" Mrs. Olly corrected with a chuckle.

World Book Day was another highly anticipated event. Students and teachers alike would come to school dressed as their favorite literary characters. Nathan's all-time favorite book was "Harry Potter," so naturally, he dressed as Harry, complete with a lightning bolt scar and round glasses.

The day was filled with activities, including a parade of costumes, a book swap, and a reading marathon in the library. Nathan's highlight was the character contest. When it was his turn to present, he pulled out a wand and recited a spell that made a puff of glitter explode from his hand.

"Expelliarmus!" he shouted, to the applause and laughter of his classmates.

Mrs. Olly, dressed as Mary Poppins, awarded Nathan a prize for "Most Enthusiastic Wizard," which he proudly added to his growing collection of quirky awards.

MIDDLE SCHOOL TRIALS

International Day was a grand celebration of diversity. Each class represented a different country, and students learned about customs, traditions, and histories. This event was a full-day affair, with performances, food stalls, and cultural displays taking over the school grounds.

Nathan's class had been assigned Italy, and he couldn't have been happier. They decorated their booth with Italian flags, pictures of famous landmarks, and even a mini Colosseum made of cardboard. The food was the real highlight, though. Nathan's mom had helped him make a massive tray of lasagna, and it was gone within minutes.

The performances were the best part. There were traditional dances, songs, and even a fashion show. Nathan's class performed a reenactment of a traditional Italian wedding, complete with Gabe playing the role of the priest and Zack as the overenthusiastic groom. Nathan, playing a guest, had to resist the urge to laugh through the entire performance.

Apart from the big events, there were numerous other non-school activity days that kept things interesting. Sports days, talent shows, and even a Science Fair had their own special place in Nathan's heart.

On Sports Day, the entire school gathered for a series of fun and competitive events. Nathan's favorite was the three-legged race, where he and Zack, despite falling down multiple times, managed to cross the finish line laughing hysterically.

The talent show was another highlight. Nathan played the piano, and though he hit a few wrong notes, the applause and cheers from his friends made him feel like a superstar.

Nathan's middle school experience was richly colored by these extracurricular activities. They provided a welcome break from the routine of classes and homework, offering a chance to learn new things, make memories, and have fun. Whether it was the thrill of scoring a goal, the joy of sharing food from different cultures, or the pride of performing in front of his peers, these events added a vibrant thread to the tapestry of his school life.

As Nathan looked forward to high school, he knew that these experiences had helped shape him. They had taught him the value of teamwork, the importance of cultural awareness, and the joy of discovering new interests. And most importantly, they had given him stories to tell and memories to cherish for a lifetime.

Chapter 11: Navigating School Politics: The Election Extravaganza

Middle school wasn't just about classes, cafeteria catastrophes, and cultural celebrations; it was also a hotbed of school politics. Nathan found himself caught up in the whirlwind of elections for Head Boy, Head Girl, prefects, and the student council, navigating this new and often comical world with his characteristic blend of curiosity and awkwardness.

The announcement of the Head Boy and Head Girl elections was met with a mixture of excitement and dread. Candidates had to be nominated, campaign, and give speeches in front of the entire school. Nathan, who preferred to stay out of the limelight, was content to watch from the sidelines. However, his friend Zack had other ideas.

"Nathan, you'd make a great Head Boy! You should totally run!" Zack exclaimed one day.

"Me? Are you kidding? I can barely remember to tie my shoelaces," Nathan replied, shaking his head.

But Zack was relentless. "Come on, it'll be fun! Plus, you get to give a speech. Imagine that!"

The thought of giving a speech in front of the whole school made Nathan's stomach churn. He admired the brave souls who put their names forward. There was Sarah, the smartest girl in class, who was running for Head Girl, and Jake, the class clown, who had somehow decided he was leadership material.

Campaign week was a blur of posters, slogans, and last-minute bribes of candy bars. Sarah's campaign was all about academic excellence and inclusivity, while Jake's slogan was "More Fun, Less Homework!" Nathan watched in amusement as Jake handed out lollipops with his face on them.

Elections for prefects were slightly less intense but still a significant part of school life. Prefects were responsible for maintaining discipline and helping out with school events. Nathan decided to give it a shot, thinking it might look good on his high school applications.

To his surprise, he was nominated by his classmates. His campaign strategy was simple: be himself. He made a few posters with the help of his artistic friend Gabe, and he even handed out some homemade cookies, which were a big hit.

On election day, Nathan gave a short speech that went something like this: "Hi, I'm Nathan. I promise not to be a bossy prefect. Vote for me if you want someone who actually listens."

He won by a landslide. His approachability and genuine demeanor had won over his peers.

The student council was the real power center of the school. They organized events, liaised with teachers, and generally made important decisions about student life. Nathan was curious about the inner workings of the council, so he decided to run for a position as a class representative.

The competition was fierce. His main rival was Chloe, a girl known for her persuasive skills and ambition. Nathan's campaign leaned heavily on humor. His posters featured him in exaggerated superhero poses with slogans like "Vote Nathan: Your Friendly Neighborhood Rep" and "Nathan: Making Middle School Bearable Since Day One."

MIDDLE SCHOOL TRIALS

During the debates, Chloe presented well-researched points and detailed plans, while Nathan took a different approach. "We need more fun and less stress. Who's with me?" he declared, to the cheers of his classmates. In the end, it was a close race, but Nathan's down-to-earth charm won him the position.

Being part of the student council was an eye-opener for Nathan. Meetings were a mix of serious discussions and hilarious mishaps. There was the time when Jake, now the treasurer, accidentally spent the entire bake sale fund on an oversized inflatable duck for the school pool party. The council had to scramble to organize another fundraiser, which ended up being more successful than the first.

Nathan found himself mediating between conflicting ideas, organizing events, and even giving presentations to the school administration. His favorite project was the "Stress-Free Week," which included yoga sessions, a petting zoo, and an ice cream social.

Nathan's foray into school politics taught him valuable lessons about leadership, teamwork, and the importance of a good sense of humor. He discovered that being a leader wasn't about being the loudest or the most popular, but about listening, being fair, and sometimes, just being able to make people laugh.

As Nathan looked back on his experiences with a smile. He had navigated the treacherous waters of school elections, survived the chaos of student council meetings, and even managed to organize a few successful events. He wasn't sure if politics was in his future, but he knew he'd carry these memories with him wherever he went.

Chapter 12: Handling rumors and gossip

Middle school drama was like navigating a maze blindfolded—full of unexpected twists, dead ends, and the occasional surprise party you didn't even know you were invited to. For Nathan, rumors, conflicts, and the wild world of social media became an adventure filled with laughter, lessons, and maybe a few face palm moments.

One fateful Monday morning, Nathan found himself at the center of a rumor so outrageous it could have been scripted for a daytime soap opera. According to a WhatsApp message that spread faster than a meme in a group chat, Nathan had supposedly whisked his classmate, Emily, away on a clandestine date to the local arcade. The rumor mill was abuzz with screenshots of blurry selfies that could have been anyone with a passing resemblance to Nathan and Emily.

"Wait, what?" Nathan exclaimed, staring at his phone in disbelief as notifications flooded in like a digital tidal wave. "I didn't even know Emily liked arcades!"

Armed with his quick wit and a healthy dose of skepticism, Nathan decided to tackle the rumor head-on. Instead of getting defensive or disappearing into the digital abyss, he took to the group chat with a burst of humor.

"Guys, hate to break it to you, but last I checked, Emily and I were busy solving algebra problems, not sipping milkshakes at the arcade," Nathan messaged, adding a winking emoji for good measure.

His response sparked a flurry of laughing emojis and relieved messages from classmates who had secretly been wondering how Nathan managed to juggle middle school drama and arcade dates without anyone noticing.

As rumors continued to circulate like wildfire through the digital grapevine, Nathan faced another challenge: managing the fallout with Emily and their circle of friends. He knew that rumors could strain even the strongest of friendships, turning lunchtime banter into awkward silences.

"Emily," Nathan began cautiously during lunch, where pizza slices and unopened juice boxes were the only witnesses to their conversation, "I swear on my Minecraft collection that I had no idea about this rumor until today."

Emily, her eyebrows raised in a mixture of amusement and annoyance, nodded in understanding. "I figured as much," she replied, reaching for a slice of pepperoni pizza. "It's ridiculous, but I'm glad you set the record straight."

With a shared laugh and a pact to ignore future rumors as creatively as possible, Nathan and Emily emerged from the drama stronger than ever, armed with a newfound appreciation for pizza and the power of friendship in the face of middle school chaos.

Through the whirlwind of rumors and group chat hysteria, Nathan learned valuable lessons about the impact of social media on teenage friendships and reputations. He realized that behind every viral message and screenshot was a person—complete with quirks, miscommunications, and the occasional embarrassing rumor that spread faster than a TikTok dance challenge.

"Guys," Nathan joked during a rare moment of calm in the group chat, "can we all agree to fact-check before we start spreading rumors? I mean, I haven't even mastered my algebra homework, let alone planning secret arcade dates."

His friends, amused by Nathan's ability to turn drama dilemmas into comedy gold, agreed wholeheartedly. They vowed to approach social media with caution and to rely on laughter to navigate the digital minefield of middle school life.

As Nathan reflected on his journey through the drama-filled halls of middle school, he realized that handling rumors, managing conflicts, and understanding social media weren't just challenges—they were opportunities for growth and a lot of laughs. Armed with his unique blend of humor, honesty, and a smartphone filled with questionable group chat messages, Nathan faced each day with a grin and a readiness to turn drama dilemmas into comedic gold.

Managing Conflicts with Friends were like navigating a maze without a map—full of twists, dead ends, and the occasional surprising shortcut. When disagreements arose over who got the last slice of cafeteria pizza, Nathan turned to his trusty arsenal of humor and diplomacy. "Guys, guys," Nathan would interject during heated debates over Minecraft strategies, "let's settle this like civilized gamers—rock, paper, scissors, lizard, Spock!"

His friends, momentarily distracted by the absurdity of the suggestion, would often dissolve into laughter and forget what they were arguing about in the first place. Nathan's knack for diffusing tensions with a well-timed joke became legendary, earning him the unofficial title of "Peacekeeper of the Lunch Table."

In the age of Instagram filters and TikTok trends, Nathan learned that social media wasn't just a platform—it was a digital battlefield where likes, comments, and emojis waged wars of popularity. From navigating the pitfalls of accidentally liking a photo from three years ago to deciphering cryptic group chat emojis that seemed to change meaning hourly, Nathan found himself in a whirlwind of virtual drama.

MIDDLE SCHOOL TRIALS

"Did you see Becky's latest TikTok dance?" his friend would ask, thrusting a smartphone into Nathan's hands. "Ah, yes," Nathan would reply, pretending to understand the intricacies of dance moves that resembled interpretive juggling more than anything else. "She's really... expressive."

Through humorous mishaps and unexpected viral moments (like the time Nathan accidentally became a meme for wearing his backpack backwards on Picture Day), Nathan discovered that social media was both a tool for connection and a playground for misunderstanding. He learned to navigate the virtual landscape with caution and a healthy dose of self-deprecating humor, realizing that behind every screen was a person—quirks, memes, and all.

Middle school might have been a roller coaster of rumors and digital pitfalls, but Nathan emerged with a newfound understanding of friendship, social dynamics, and the power of laughter to navigate even the wildest of teenage adventures. As he looked ahead to high school, he knew that with humor as his shield and emojis as his secret weapon, there were no drama dilemmas he couldn't handle—arcade date rumors and all.

Chapter 13: The Roller Coaster of Puberty

One moment Nathan was comfortably fitting into his favorite pair of jeans, and the next, they were halfway up his calves. Puberty hit him like a surprise pop quiz, leaving him scrambling to adjust to a body that seemed determined to outgrow his wardrobe overnight.

"Seriously, do these jeans shrink every time I blink?" Nathan joked, tugging at the hemlines in futile attempts to conceal his ever-lengthening limbs.

His once-reliable mirror became a source of existential crisis as he tried to reconcile the image of a gangly teenager with the memory of his shorter, less limbs-to-trip-over self. "I swear," he quipped to his reflection, "I must be growing taller at the speed of a runaway giraffe."

Emotions became another battleground as Nathan navigated the hormonal roller coaster ride that came with puberty. From inexplicable bursts of laughter during math class to sudden bouts of melancholy over forgotten lunchbox snacks, Nathan felt like his emotions had developed a mind of their own.

"Today's mood: emotionally confused with a side of existential angst," Nathan announced to his friends, who chuckled in solidarity, each grappling with their own hormonal hurricanes.

Navigating friendships became trickier as mood swings threatened to turn innocent disagreements into full-blown drama storms. Nathan learned to ride out emotional waves with humor and patience, often diffusing tense moments with a well-timed joke or a shared eye roll over algebra equations that seemed as perplexing as his changing emotions.

MIDDLE SCHOOL TRIALS

Alongside physical changes came the uninvited guests of puberty: acne and body image blues. Nathan's once-smooth complexion became a battleground of erupting pimples that seemed to have a personal vendetta against school picture days and social events. "Behold," Nathan quipped, pointing to a particularly defiant pimple on his chin, "the latest addition to my face's modern art collection."

Despite his humor, Nathan struggled with self-consciousness as he compared himself to classmates who seemed untouched by puberty's quirky sense of humor. He learned the art of concealing acne with strategic hoodie placements and mastering the art of self-deprecating jokes that turned insecurities into punchlines.

As Nathan weathered the storm of puberty's physical and emotional challenges, he discovered hidden reserves of resilience and self-acceptance. He realized that self-esteem wasn't about flawless skin or perfectly timed growth spurts—it was about embracing imperfections with grace and finding confidence in the midst of change.

"Maybe my jeans don't fit perfectly," Nathan admitted to himself one morning, staring at his reflection with newfound appreciation, "but neither does anyone else's journey through puberty."

With each passing day and awkward encounter with puberty's surprises, Nathan learned to laugh at the absurdity, find strength in vulnerability, and navigate middle school with a sense of humor as his compass. He discovered that puberty wasn't just about physical changes—it was a rite of passage that tested his resilience and shaped him into a more confident, empathetic young adult.

On his journey through puberty in middle school, he realized that while the road was bumpy and filled with unexpected detours, it was also a transformative period of self-discovery and growth. Armed with humor, resilience, and a newfound appreciation for the quirks of adolescence, Nathan faced each day with a sense of humor and a readiness to embrace whatever changes puberty threw his way.

Middle school might have been a battleground of body changes and self-esteem challenges, but Nathan emerged stronger and more confident, ready to tackle the next chapter of his journey with a grin and the assurance that even runaway growth spurts couldn't derail his resilience.

Chapter 14: Handling family conflicts

Navigating family dynamics in middle school was like playing a never-ending game of charades with unpredictable teammates and an audience of critics who knew your embarrassing childhood stories by heart. For Nathan, communicating with parents and siblings, balancing family expectations with personal goals, and handling occasional conflicts became a comedic adventure filled with laughter, lessons, and maybe a few eye-rolling moments.

Communication with parents was a delicate dance of decoding parental expressions and mastering the art of selective disclosure. From deciphering the meaning behind a raised eyebrow during report card season to navigating the minefield of curfew negotiations, Nathan learned that honesty paired with humor was often the best strategy.

"Mom, Dad," Nathan announced with mock solemnity, "I come bearing news of a B+ in math. Please hold the applause." His parents exchanged amused glances before launching into a round of exaggerated cheers that echoed through the house, signaling Nathan's mastery of the art of report card diplomacy.

Siblings added an extra layer of unpredictability to family dynamics. From negotiating bathroom schedules that rivaled international peace treaties to settling disputes over who ate the last slice of pizza, Nathan and his siblings mastered the art of sibling banter that veered from playful teasing to full-blown prank wars.

Finding the balance between family expectations and personal goals often felt like juggling flaming torches while balancing on a unicycle—exciting, nerve-wracking, and occasionally singed by unexpected plot twists. Nathan navigated the tightrope of academic ambitions and extracurricular passions with a mix of determination and self-deprecating humor.

"Sorry, Mom," Nathan quipped after missing a high note during his piano recital, "apparently, I didn't inherit the family's musical genes. Can I interest you in a dramatic rendition of 'Chopsticks' instead?"

Despite the occasional mismatch between family expectations and Nathan's budding interests in soccer and stand-up comedy, he learned that open communication and compromise were the keys to finding harmony amidst the chaos of middle school ambitions.

Nathan's battles with his parents often centered around the classic showdowns of chores versus video game time or the eternal struggle of bedtime versus Netflix marathons. Arguments over the importance of finishing homework versus the urgency of defeating virtual dragons in his favorite game became epic battles of wills that tested Nathan's negotiation skills and comedic timing.

"Dad, hear me out," Nathan pleaded during a heated debate over his curfew. "If time is a social construct, shouldn't bedtime be, too? I'm just exploring the boundaries of temporal theory here."

His father, trying to suppress a smile, countered with a well-worn lecture on responsibility and the importance of sleep. Nathan, undeterred, responded with a PowerPoint presentation titled "The Scientific Benefits of Late-Night Gaming" that included dubious statistics and a surprising number of animated GIFs.

One battle Nathan couldn't win was the legendary Sleepover Saga of 'Middle School Mayhem.' Armed with persuasive arguments about friendship, trust, and the necessity of late-night pizza consumption, Nathan approached his parents with a proposal for the ultimate sleepover extravaganza.

MIDDLE SCHOOL TRIALS

"Come on, Mom, Dad," Nathan pleaded, his eyes wide with the enthusiasm only a middle schooler planning an all-night gaming marathon could muster. "It's just one night of harmless fun. What could possibly go wrong?"

His parents exchanged a knowing glance that spoke volumes about their memories of youthful escapades and the inevitable chaos that followed. "Nathan," his mom began, a hint of amusement in her voice, "we appreciate your enthusiasm, but sleepovers are like potato chips—you always end up wanting more than just one."

Defeated but undeterred, Nathan retreated with a sigh, his dreams of gaming conquests and epic pillow fights postponed for another day. Though disappointed, he learned that even in the face of parental veto, there was humor to be found in negotiating curfews and compromising on the definition of "harmless fun."

As Nathan reflected on his adventures in family matters during middle school, he realized that while navigating parental expectations, sibling antics, and occasional conflicts required patience and negotiation, it also provided moments of laughter and lessons in resilience.

Middle school wasn't just about surviving family dynamics—it was about embracing the quirks, sharing laughter, and learning to communicate with humor and honesty. Armed with a newfound appreciation for the comedic side of family life, Nathan faced each day with a grin and the knowledge that even the most chaotic family moments could be turned into memorable chapters of his middle school journey.

Chapter 15: Crushes and First Loves

Middle school crushes were like trying to solve a Rubik's Cube blindfolded—confusing, frustrating, and occasionally filled with surprising moments of success. For Nathan, navigating feelings for the first time, dealing with rejection, and understanding the complexities of healthy relationships became a comedic journey of heart-fluttering moments, awkward encounters, and lessons in love that were as unpredictable as a cafeteria food fight.

When Nathan first laid eyes on Sarah from across the classroom, it was as if someone had hit the pause button on the chaos of middle school life—a moment frozen in time where his heart did cartwheels like an over-caffeinated acrobat, while his brain stumbled through a mental obstacle course of awkwardness.

His attempts at suave conversation were as graceful as a newborn giraffe learning to walk. "Hey, Sarah," Nathan blurted out one day, his voice cracking like an adolescent choir boy trying to hit a high note. "Did you know that statistically speaking, there's a 97.8% chance you're the reason my algebra homework has turned into a love letter to quadratic equations?"

Sarah blinked, clearly taken aback by the unexpected blend of math and metaphorical romance. Nathan, undeterred by his own verbal mishap, continued with an awkward smile that could have powered a small city with its sheer wattage of nervous energy.

"And, um, did you know," Nathan added hastily, trying to recover from his initial stumble, "that your smile is like a ray of sunshine that brightens even the gloomiest days of quadratic equations?"

MIDDLE SCHOOL TRIALS

Sarah's expression softened into a bemused smile, her eyes betraying a mix of amusement and genuine curiosity. Nathan mentally high-fived himself for not tripping over his own shoelaces during what felt like the most epic verbal adventure of his middle school career.

As Nathan navigated the uncharted waters of crush-induced word vomit and strategic lunchroom seating arrangements, he discovered that even in the midst of his own awkwardness, there was humor to be found. From accidentally quoting Shakespeare while trying to compliment Sarah's hair to mistaking a potted plant for a good-luck charm during a nerve-wracking math quiz, Nathan embraced the comedy of errors that came with navigating his first crush.

Through it all, Nathan learned that while crushes might start with heart-fluttering moments and clumsy compliments, true connections were built on shared laughter, genuine conversations, and the occasional mutual eye roll over cafeteria food choices that could only be described as culinary experiments gone wrong.

Of course, not every crush ended with a slow-motion walk into the sunset accompanied by a soundtrack of romantic ballads. When Nathan finally mustered the courage to confess his feelings to Sarah, her response was as unexpected as a surprise pop quiz on a Friday afternoon.

"Nathan," Sarah began gently, her voice carrying the weight of unspoken kindness, "you're sweet, but I think we're better off as friends." Nathan's heart sank faster than a lead balloon in physics class. "Right," he replied with a forced grin that felt more like a grimace. "Just friends. Got it."

As he navigated the post-rejection slump, Nathan found solace in the universal truth that ice cream and reruns of goofy sitcoms were the ultimate antidote to a broken heart.

ROSEANNE GODKIN

"Who knew," Nathan joked with his friends during a lunchtime debate on the merits of mystery meat sandwiches, "that the key to a successful relationship could be as simple as agreeing on pizza toppings?"

As Nathan navigated the complexities of friendship and the occasional crush, he realized that laughter was the secret ingredient to understanding healthy relationships—whether it was with friends, crushes, or the occasional awkward encounter with a lunchroom crush.

Middle school crushes weren't just about butterflies and heartache—they were about embracing the awkwardness, sharing laughter, and learning to appreciate the quirks that made every crush and rejection a stepping stone in Nathan's journey of love and self-discovery. Armed with a newfound appreciation for mathematical romance and the comedic side of crushes, Nathan faced each day with a grin and the knowledge that even the most awkward moments could be turned into memorable chapters of his middle school journey.

Chapter 16: Weekend Whirlwinds and Break-Time Bonanzas

Middle school wasn't just about surviving classes and school politics; it was also about what happened outside of school. For Nathan, weekends, playdates, camping trips, and school breaks were an eclectic mix of family time, adventures with friends, and the occasional disaster that provided endless entertainment.

Nathan's weekends with his family were never boring. They were a series of unexpected events, awkward moments, and hilarious misadventures.

Take Saturday mornings, for instance. Nathan's mom had a strict "family breakfast" rule. This meant everyone had to be at the table by 8:00 AM, bright-eyed and bushy-tailed. Of course, for Nathan, being bright-eyed at that hour was a challenge.

One Saturday, in his half-awake state, Nathan poured orange juice into his cereal instead of milk. The look on his face when he took the first bite was priceless. His dad, suppressing laughter, asked, "How's that new breakfast combo working out for you, champ?"

Then there were the family outings. One memorable weekend, they decided to go on a family hike. Nathan, ever the skeptic, had packed enough snacks to feed a small army. Halfway through the hike, when they encountered a rather steep hill, his sisters, Emma and Amy, decided they had had enough and staged a sit-in protest right there on the trail. Nathan, munching on his third Kellogg bar, couldn't help but laugh as his parents tried to coax them to move.

Nathan's playdates with his friends were legendary for their sheer unpredictability. Whether it was Zack, Gabe, or the whole gang, there was always something going on.

One time, Zack invited Nathan over for a playdate that quickly turned into an epic Nerf gun battle. The living room became a war zone, complete with forts made out of couch cushions and strategic snack breaks. Nathan's tactical genius was on full display when he ambushed Zack from behind the recliner, only to trip over a stray Lego and face-plant into a pile of stuffed animals.

Another classic playdate involved a science experiment gone wrong. Gabe had seen a YouTube video about making a glitter and dish soap "explosion." They decided to recreate it but added their twist by mixing in various kitchen ingredients.

The recipe was simple enough: fill a bottle with water, add glitter, dish soap, and then mix. The idea was to create a mesmerizing lava lamp effect. However, Nathan and Gabe decided that more was more, so they added extra glitter and dish soap to make the effect "epic."

The mixture, instead of creating a calm, swirling lava lamp, turned into a foamy, glittery geyser. The bottle overflowed, and soon, the kitchen floor was covered in soap suds and glitter. Nathan's mom walked in just as Gabe slipped and fell, creating a slow-motion effect that ended with Gabe covered in sparkles, looking like a disco ball.

"Why does it always look like a unicorn exploded in here when you two do science?" Nathan's mom asked, shaking her head but unable to hide her smile.

They spent the rest of the afternoon cleaning up, laughing about how they had "discovered" the messiest experiment ever.

MIDDLE SCHOOL TRIALS

Camping trips with schoolmates were a rite of passage, and Nathan's school organized one every year. These trips were a mix of outdoor fun, mosquito bites, and ghost stories that made you regret staying up late.

On one such trip to Rapids Camp Sagana, Nathan and his friends were excited about white water rafting. The guide, seeing their enthusiasm, decided to give them an extra thrilling ride. Nathan's heart was in his throat the whole time, especially when Zack almost fell out of the raft while trying to take a selfie. They all emerged from the river drenched but exhilarated, laughing about their "near-death experience."

At night, they gathered around the campfire for s'mores and ghost stories. Gabe, always the dramatic one, told a tale so scary that Zack insisted on sleeping with a flashlight on. Of course, Nathan couldn't resist sneaking up on Zack's tent and making spooky noises, which resulted in a hilarious scream and a few choice words that Zack's parents wouldn't approve of.

School breaks were Nathan's favorite time of year. They were an opportunity to sleep in, hang out with friends, and embark on various adventures. During one spring break, Nathan's parents decided to take a road trip to visit relatives. The journey was filled with classic road trip antics: endless rounds of "I Spy," arguments over the best snacks, and the infamous "Are we there yet?" question every five minutes. Nathan's dad tried to keep spirits high by playing cheesy 80s music, much to Nathan and Emma's horror.

Summer breaks were all about playdates and adventures. Nathan and his friends loved visiting the local swimming pool. One summer, they decided to hold an impromptu diving contest. Nathan, attempting a grand cannonball, miscalculated and ended up with a spectacular belly flop that had everyone in stitches.

Holidays were another highlight. Halloween was always a blast, with Nathan and his friends planning elaborate costumes. One year, Nathan dressed as a zombie, complete with fake blood and tattered clothes. The costume was so convincing that when he jumped out to scare Emma, she responded with a shriek that could be heard two blocks away.

Christmas break meant family gatherings, which Nathan both loved and dreaded. He enjoyed the presents and the food but had to endure his Aunt Martha's endless questions about school and his future. One year, in an attempt to avoid her, Nathan hid in the basement with a plate of cookies, only to be discovered by his grandma, who joined him and started telling embarrassing stories from his childhood.

Nathan's weekends, playdates, camping trips, and school breaks were a tapestry of chaos, fun, and learning. These experiences, filled with humor and mishaps, taught him about the importance of family, the joy of friendship, and the value of stepping outside his comfort zone. Whether he was pouring orange juice into his cereal, staging Nerf battles, or surviving belly flops, Nathan learned that life was a lot more fun when you embraced the unpredictable and laughed along the way.

Chapter 17: Navigating the Digital World

Navigating the digital world in middle school was like embarking on a virtual expedition through a maze of memes, emojis, and occasional digital detours. For Nathan, managing screen time, staying safe online, and navigating social media responsibly became a comedic journey filled with technological triumphs, occasional mishaps, and valuable lessons in digital citizenship.

Balancing screen time in the age of endless YouTube videos and addictive mobile games was a challenge that tested Nathan's self-discipline and his family's patience.

"Nathan," his mom would call out from the kitchen, "it's been three hours—did you accidentally fall into the digital rabbit hole again?" "Um, just conducting important research for a history project," Nathan would reply, frantically minimizing browser tabs that showcased cat videos and conspiracy theories about school cafeteria mystery meat.

His attempts at negotiating additional screen time often involved elaborate promises to finish chores with newfound efficiency or citing the benefits of multitasking (which usually meant watching tutorials on how to perform magic tricks while allegedly completing math assignments).

Navigating the virtual landscape came with its own set of digital potholes and parental caution signs. Nathan learned early on that not everything online was as it seemed, especially when his attempts at researching a school project on medieval armor led to accidentally stumbling upon a forum for aspiring knights in training.

"Nathan," his dad would chuckle, "did you really think you could become a knight by ordering a suit of armor online?"

Undeterred by parental skepticism, Nathan honed his online research skills, eventually becoming the go-to guru for debunking internet hoaxes and fact-checking the validity of dubious homework shortcuts touted by questionable websites.

Social media presented its own set of challenges— from mastering the art of crafting the perfect profile picture to deciphering the hidden meanings behind cryptic emojis in group chats. "Mom, Dad," Nathan would proclaim during dinner, his voice carrying the gravity of a seasoned social media analyst, "I've decoded the secret language of emojis. Apparently, a winking face followed by a ghost emoji means 'I accidentally scared the cat with my magic trick again.'"

His parents exchanged amused glances, secretly impressed by Nathan's ability to decode the digital symbols of his generation.

One of Nathan's greatest digital escapes was his love for Roblox, where virtual adventures with friends often extended into marathon sessions that rivaled the length of epic movie marathons.

"Just one more game," Nathan would declare on Saturday mornings, his enthusiasm matching the intensity of a professional gamer at a championship match. Hours would slip by unnoticed as he and his friends battled virtual enemies, built virtual empires, and occasionally broke into spontaneous dance parties in virtual clubs.

It wasn't until Sunday evening, surrounded by unfinished homework assignments and a slightly frazzled mom holding a stack of textbooks, that Nathan realized the extent of his digital immersion. "Nathan," his mom would sigh, "remember that algebra project that was due tomorrow?"

MIDDLE SCHOOL TRIALS

Nathan's eyes widened in realization, his digital adventures momentarily overshadowed by the looming specter of incomplete assignments. "Oops," he muttered sheepishly, mentally drafting an apology to quadratic equations everywhere.

Nathan's digital adventures weren't without consequences, especially when his screen time encroached upon shared family spaces and sparked sibling rivalries that rivaled the Clash of Clans.

"Hey, Nathan," his younger sister would protest, interrupting his epic Roblox quest with the ferocity of a warrior princess defending her digital turf, "you promised to help me with my science project!"

Caught between the allure of virtual conquests and the reality of sibling warfare, Nathan navigated the delicate balance of family dynamics with a mix of negotiation tactics and the occasional strategic retreat to his digital fortress.

Navigating the digital world also meant confronting the occasional skirmish with teachers over unfinished projects that mysteriously vanished into the black hole of online distractions. "Nathan," his math teacher would sigh, peering over a stack of overdue assignments, "where's your algebra project on geometric proofs?"

Caught between the guilt of procrastination and the allure of digital diversions, Nathan attempted to explain the intricate dance of screen time management and the gravitational pull of virtual adventures that occasionally overshadowed his academic responsibilities.

As Nathan reflected on his adventures in the digital world during middle school, he realized that while technology brought new challenges and occasional pitfalls, it also provided opportunities for creativity, connection, and personal growth. Armed with a blend of technological savvy and a knack for turning digital mishaps into moments of humor, Nathan faced each online adventure with a grin and the knowledge that navigating the digital landscape was as much about laughter as it was about learning.

Chapter 18: Misadventures in Mental Health and Wellness

Middle school was like juggling flaming torches—exciting, occasionally terrifying, and definitely prone to unexpected mishaps. For Nathan, navigating the choppy waters of adolescence meant learning some valuable lessons about mental health and wellness, often with a side of humor and a dash of self-deprecating charm.

Nathan quickly became acquainted with the telltale signs of stress and anxiety, which often manifested in ways that were both comical and concerning. From the classic "deer in headlights" look before a surprise quiz to the involuntary twitch that emerged whenever he glanced at his overflowing backpack, Nathan's body had a knack for signaling distress in the most dramatic ways possible.

"I think my eyebrow twitch is Morse code for 'help, algebra is attacking,'" Nathan would joke with his friends during lunch, his exaggerated gestures earning a mixture of laughter and sympathetic nods.

In the midst of academic turmoil and social escapades, Nathan discovered the art of coping through unconventional means. His coping mechanisms ranged from spontaneous dance parties in his room (complete with embarrassing dance moves that rivaled a malfunctioning robot) to adopting a strict regimen of "study breaks" that suspiciously coincided with the release of his favorite video game updates.

"Guys," Nathan proclaimed during a particularly intense study session turned impromptu dance-off, "I've found that the key to surviving middle school stress is a strategic combination of terrible dance moves and strategic snack raids in the kitchen. Works every time!"

His friends, caught between amusement and admiration for Nathan's ability to turn stress relief into a performance art, eagerly joined in, creating memories that blurred the lines between chaos and camaraderie.

Amid the laughter and dance-induced endorphins, Nathan also learned the importance of recognizing when to seek help. Whether it was confiding in his drama teacher about stage fright before the school play or scheduling a heartfelt conversation with his mom about the complexities of navigating crushes and friendships, Nathan discovered that vulnerability and humor were a powerful duo in tackling life's challenges.

"Mom," Nathan would confess over a batch of freshly baked cookies that were definitely meant for stress relief rather than nutrition, "I think I may need some advice on how to decode the mysteries of algebra and the even greater mysteries of middle school friendships."

His mom would listen with a mix of empathy and amusement, secretly marveling at Nathan's ability to blend self-awareness with a healthy dose of humor in moments of uncertainty.

As Nathan reflected on his misadventures in mental health and wellness, he realized that middle school was less about finding perfect solutions and more about embracing the journey with resilience and laughter. Armed with an arsenal of terrible dance moves, cookie-fueled confessions, and the unwavering support of friends and family, Nathan faced each day with a grin and a willingness to tackle life's ups and downs head-on.

MIDDLE SCHOOL TRIALS

Middle school had taught him that navigating stress and anxiety was as much about embracing imperfection as it was about discovering personal strength. With a newfound appreciation for the comedic side of self-care and a repertoire of dance moves that defied all logic, Nathan looked forward to high school, knowing that his journey toward mental well-being was a continuous adventure worth experiencing with humor and heart.

Chapter 19: High School, Here We Come

As middle school drew to a close, Nathan found himself on the brink of a new adventure: High school. With a mixture of excitement and trepidation, he began setting his sights on the future, crafting plans that balanced short-term goals, long-term dreams, and a healthy dose of optimism. High school was looming large on the horizon, and Nathan was determined to face it head-on, with a bit of humor and a lot of heart.

Nathan knew that success in high school would require more than just surviving the cafeteria and avoiding awkward social interactions. It was time to get serious about setting goals—both the ones that would get him through the next semester and the ones that would guide him toward his dreams.

Short-term goals included mastering the art of not losing his homework in the black hole that was his backpack and finally figuring out how to write a lab report that didn't resemble a grocery list. Long-term goals, on the other hand, were a bit more ambitious.

"I'm going to join the debate team," Nathan declared to his friends, who were more used to his proclamations about video game strategies than academic aspirations. "And maybe the drama club. And definitely avoid getting lost on the way to class."

His friends nodded, offering supportive cheers and advice that ranged from "never underestimate the power of a well-organized binder" to "always have a spare snack hidden in your locker."

MIDDLE SCHOOL TRIALS

Preparation for high school went beyond just academic readiness; it was about mentally gearing up for a new environment filled with new faces, new challenges, and, of course, new opportunities for embarrassing moments.

As Nathan prepared for high school, he found himself facing one of the most important decisions of his academic journey: choosing subjects that would shape his future. With a budding ambition to become a computer analyst, Nathan knew that his choices needed to align with his long-term goals. Fortunately, he had the support of his parents and teachers to help guide him through this critical process.

Nathan's parents were thrilled to see him so enthusiastic about his future career. They arranged a family meeting one evening, complete with snacks and a stack of high school course catalogs.

"Nathan, choosing the right subjects now can set you up for success in college and your future career," his mom said, spreading out the course catalogs on the dining table. "Let's look at the options and see what aligns with your goal of becoming a computer analyst."

His dad nodded in agreement, adding, "It's important to balance your interests with subjects that will challenge you and build the skills you need."

Nathan, armed with a highlighter and a notepad, began to sift through the options. Math, science, and technology courses stood out immediately.

To get additional insights, Nathan scheduled a meeting with his school counselor, Mr. Mann, who was known for his expertise in guiding students through their academic choices.

"Nathan, it's great that you have a clear career goal in mind," Mr. Mann said, his office adorned with motivational posters and college pennants.

"Let's look at the courses that will best prepare you for a career in computer analysis."

He pulled out a list of recommended courses, highlighting subjects like Computer Science, Advanced Mathematics, Physics, and even some electives in coding and software development.

"These courses will give you a strong foundation in the skills you'll need," he explained. "But don't forget to include some humanities and social sciences to keep a well-rounded perspective. Critical thinking and communication are just as important in the tech world."

Nathan's parents and Mr. Mann helped him create a balanced schedule that included the essential courses for his future career while also allowing room for personal interests and extracurricular activities.

"Okay," Nathan said, ticking off the courses on his notepad. "I'll take Computer Science, Advanced Math, and Physics for sure. Maybe I can add an elective in Digital Art to mix things up?"

His mom smiled. "That sounds like a great plan. Remember to stay flexible and open to exploring new interests. High school is a time to discover what you're passionate about."

Nathan's excitement grew as he realized how his high school courses would set the stage for his dream of becoming a computer analyst. He made a commitment to stay motivated and work hard, knowing that his efforts now would pay off in the future.

"Just think," Nathan mused aloud to his parents one evening, "in a few years, I'll be creating software that could change the world, or at least make life a bit easier for people."

His dad patted him on the back. "And it all starts with the choices you're making now. Keep dreaming big and stay focused."

MIDDLE SCHOOL TRIALS

With the guidance of his parents and teachers, Nathan felt confident and excited about his high school journey. He knew that the subjects he chose would not only prepare him for college but also set him on the path to achieving his dream of becoming a computer analyst. Embracing the support and advice from those around him, Nathan looked forward to the challenges and opportunities ahead, ready to turn his ambitions into reality.

Beyond the logistics and the daily grind, Nathan knew that high school was a time to dream big and stay motivated. Whether it was aspiring to make the honor roll, imagining himself as the lead in the school play, or fantasizing about acing every exam, Nathan allowed himself to dream, setting his sights on a future filled with possibilities.

"High school is just the beginning," he told himself one night, staring at the ceiling and imagining the epic adventures that awaited him. "I'm going to make the most of it, one awkward encounter at a time."

To keep himself motivated, Nathan created a vision board that combined academic goals, personal milestones, and a few humorous reminders not to take life too seriously. It featured everything from college brochures and inspiring quotes to pictures of his favorite comedians and a list of "Top Ten Ways to Survive High School Drama."

"Dream big," his vision board proclaimed, "but always keep a stash of emergency chocolate for those inevitable rough days."

As Nathan prepared to step into the uncharted territory of high school, he realized that his journey was about more than just achieving goals—it was about embracing each moment with confidence, humor, and a willingness to learn from every experience. With a clear vision of his future, the support of friends and family, and an unwavering belief in his ability to navigate whatever came his way, Nathan faced the transition with a smile and a sense of adventure.

High school was sure to bring its fair share of challenges and triumphs, but Nathan was ready. Armed with short-term strategies, long-term dreams, and a knack for finding humor in every situation, he stepped into his future with excitement and optimism, knowing that the best was yet to come.

Chapter 20: The Last Day of Middle School

The last day of middle school was a whirlwind of emotions for Nathan and his classmates. The hallways buzzed with a mix of excitement and nostalgia, punctuated by the occasional squeal of a locker being cleaned out for the last time. Nathan walked through the halls, savoring every moment, every face, and every corner of the school that had been his second home for the past few years.

As the final bell rang, the students filed into the auditorium for the farewell assembly. The air was thick with anticipation. Principal Allen, known for his inspiring speeches and occasional dad jokes, stood on the stage, ready to send them off with a memorable farewell.

"Students, today marks the end of one chapter and the beginning of another," Principal Allen began, his voice echoing through the room. "You've survived pop quizzes, cafeteria food fights, and even my legendary science tests. You've grown not just in height—seriously, some of you shot up like weeds—but also in wisdom and character."

The crowd chuckled, and Nathan couldn't help but grin. He glanced at his friends, remembering their shared adventures and misadventures.

Various teachers stepped forward to offer their parting advice, each one adding a unique blend of wisdom and humor. Ms. Smith, the math teacher, took the stage first. "Always show your work," she advised, waving a calculator in the air. "Because even calculators can be wrong, and also, they don't appreciate it when you throw them at the wall in frustration."

Ms. Grimsby, the English teacher, followed with her trademark enthusiasm. "A well-placed semicolon can change your life," she said, dramatically pausing mid-sentence. "And remember, don't let your sentences run on like that one time I forgot to stop talking about Shakespeare."

Coach Davis, the games teacher, was next. "Keep moving, whether it's on the track or through life," he said, flexing his muscles for emphasis. "And if you're ever in doubt, just remember: running away from your problems burns more calories than sitting around worrying about them."

Each piece of advice was met with laughter and applause, as the students enjoyed the lighthearted but heartfelt messages from their teachers.

Then came the much-anticipated prize-giving ceremony. Awards ranged from the serious to the downright silly, each one celebrating the unique quirks and talents of the students.

"Nathan Moore, please come up to receive your award," called out Principal Allen.

Nathan made his way to the stage, slightly bewildered but curious. To his surprise, he was handed a small trophy labeled "Most Likely to Accidentally Start a Science Experiment in the Cafeteria."

Nathan accepted it with a sheepish smile, recalling the day his vinegar and baking soda project had erupted all over the lunch tables. The audience erupted in laughter and applause as Nathan gave a mock bow. His friends received their own awards. Zack was dubbed "Class Clown Extraordinaire," a title he accepted with a comedic flourish. Gabe received the "Most Likely to Win a Nobel Prize" award, which he accepted with a shy smile, already plotting how he could live up to that title.

MIDDLE SCHOOL TRIALS

Principal Allen took the stage one last time to close the ceremony with his final words of wisdom.

"Remember, middle school has prepared you for the journey ahead. High school will have its own challenges, but you've got the skills and the spirit to tackle anything. And if all else fails, just remember: no one expects you to know how to dance at prom. Just have fun and don't trip over your own feet!"

With that, the students erupted in applause, cheering and hugging as they realized they were officially done with middle school.

As the assembly ended, the students spilled out into the hallways, where they took their time saying their goodbyes. Nathan found himself surrounded by friends, each reminiscing about their favorite middle school moments.

"Remember that time we all got detention for the food fight?" Zack said, laughing. "And then Nathan tried to clean it up with a mop that was too big for him?"

They all laughed, feeling the bittersweet mix of endings and new beginnings. Nathan looked around at his friends, realizing just how much they had all grown together.

Chapter 21: Prom Night and Future Plans

Prom night was the talk of the school for weeks. Nathan was particularly excited because he had mustered the courage to ask Sarah to be his date. To his delight, she had said yes.

"Nathan, I can't believe you're going to prom with Sarah!" his sister teased. "Just make sure you don't trip over your own shoelaces."

With a mix of nerves and excitement, Nathan prepared for the big night. He donned a slightly too-big suit (courtesy of his dad's old prom attire) and tried to tame his unruly hair. His mom beamed with pride, snapping pictures like a paparazzo.

The gymnasium had been transformed into a sparkling wonderland, with twinkling lights, colorful decorations, and a dance floor that seemed to beckon them all. Tables were laden with a feast that included everything from mini sandwiches and chicken nuggets to an extravagant dessert table featuring a chocolate fountain and an array of sweets.

Nathan and Sarah entered the gym, their eyes wide with awe. The room buzzed with excitement as classmates mingled, danced, and laughed. The DJ played a mix of the latest hits and nostalgic middle school anthems, creating an atmosphere that was both energetic and sentimental.

"Nathan, this place looks amazing!" Sarah exclaimed, her eyes sparkling as they made their way to the dance floor.

MIDDLE SCHOOL TRIALS

"Yeah, it's like stepping into a fairy tale," Nathan agreed, feeling a mixture of pride and nervousness.

They danced to upbeat songs, attempting their best (and sometimes hilariously awkward) moves. Nathan's friends joined in, turning the dance floor into a scene of joyous chaos. There were group dances, solo performances that drew cheers, and slow dances that made everyone sigh with the sweetness of young love.

As the night wore on, Nathan and his friends took a moment to sit down and enjoy the feast. They piled their plates with snacks and desserts, laughing and reminiscing about their middle school adventures.

"Remember that time we had the epic food fight in the cafeteria?" Gabe asked, causing everyone to burst into laughter.

"And how about when we tried to start a band and realized none of us could actually play instruments?" Zack added, grinning.

"And how about when we built that epic volcano for the science fair?" Gabe added. "Nathan, you're the only person I know who could turn a project into a natural disaster."

The memories flowed freely, each story a testament to the bond they had formed over the years. Nathan looked around the table, feeling a sense of gratitude for the friends who had been with him through thick and thin.

As the night drew to a close, the DJ announced the final song—a slow, sentimental tune that made everyone rush to the dance floor for one last dance. Nathan and Sarah swayed to the music, surrounded by their friends.

"I'm really glad I came to prom with you, Nathan," Sarah said, smiling up at him.

"Me too," Nathan replied, feeling a warmth in his chest that had nothing to do with the dance and everything to do with the moment.

Prom night was a fitting end to their middle school journey—a night filled with laughter, friendship, and the promise of more adventures to come. As Nathan looked around at his classmates, he felt a sense of optimism about the future. They had navigated middle school together, celebrating successes big and small, and now they were ready to face high school with the same spirit of camaraderie.

With the last notes of the song fading away, Nathan knew that this was just the beginning. High school awaited, filled with new challenges and triumphs. But for now, he savored the moment, surrounded by friends and feeling ready for whatever came next.

Don't miss out!

Visit the website below and you can sign up to receive emails whenever Roseanne Godkin publishes a new book. There's no charge and no obligation.

https://books2read.com/r/B-A-LUXLC-EDIDF

BOOKS 2 READ

Connecting independent readers to independent writers.

Did you love *Middle School Trials*? Then you should read *Twisty Tails: Wacky Tongue Twisters for Kids*[1] by Roseanne Godkin!

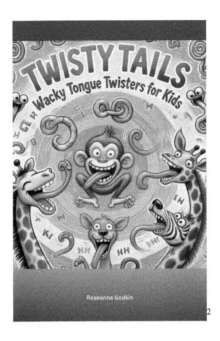

[2]

Twisty Tails: Wacky Tongue Twisters for Kids is a fun-filled adventure into the wild and wacky world of tongue twisters! From silly sounds and crazy rhymes to frisky animals and bizarre food combinations, each chapter offers new twists and turns. Kids will meet goofy goblins, tackle solo challenges, and even explore tongue twisters from around the globe.Packed with famous twisters, this book guarantees endless giggles and lots of tricky fun as readers twist their tongues in all sorts of playful ways!

---

1. https://books2read.com/u/3GJQEP

2. https://books2read.com/u/3GJQEP

Also by Roseanne Godkin

Amazing Women in Science: Breaking Boundaries
Captivating Places For Curious Kids
Mysteries Of The Hidden World
The Crap You Don't Need: The Perfect Way to Cut Toxic Ties
From Surviving to Thriving: Integrative Healing for Women's Anxiety
Unlocking the Teen Mind: A Guide for Parents and Educators
Whimsical Wonders: Magical Journeys Short Stories
Cut The Toxic Ties: A Guide to Navigating Relationships with Toxic People
Love in the Digital Twilight
Me Vs Me. A Guide for Awesome Potential Child
Unapologetically You: Breaking Free from Guilt and Shame
Apologies Unplugged: Sorry Not Sorry! Communicate with confidence
Breathe: A Mindful Approach to Managing Anxiety
Hustle & Connect: Building Your Tribe in the Digital Age
Timeless Aspirations: Embracing Your Ageless Dreams
Quit Wasting Cash: Smart Habits for Better Spending
The Healing Pen: Letters to My Past, Present, and Future
Selling Hope: Words That Matter
The Age of Annoyance: Surviving Everyday Irritations
Rainbow Inside: Learning to Understand Our Feelings
Stand Tall: A Brave Heart Guide to Bullying
Laughter & Life: Tales from the Silver Years

Twisty Tails: Wacky Tongue Twisters for Kids
Michael geht in die Schule
The Classroom and the Crib: Navigating Dual Roles
Echoes of Tomorrow: A World Rewritten by Machines
The Power of Words: Once Spoken, Never Forgotten
Middle School Trials